Founding
Vocation
& Future
Vision

FOUNDING
VOCATION
& FUTURE
VISION

*The Self-understanding
of the Disciples of Christ
and the Churches of Christ*

ANTHONY L. DUNNAVANT
RICHARD T. HUGHES
PAUL M. BLOWERS

Chalice Press ®
St. Louis, Missouri

All scripture quotations, unless otherwise indicated, are from the *New Revised Standard Version Bible*, copyright 1989, Division of Christian Education of the National Council of the Churches of Christ in the USA. Used by permission.

Scripture quotations marked (NIV) are taken from the HOLY BIBLE, NEW INTERNATIONAL VERSION®. NIV®. Copyright© 1973, 1978, 1984 by International Bible Society. Used by permission of Zondervan Publishing House. All rights reserved.

Cover Design: Grady Gunter
Cover Illustration: Michael Domínguez
Interior design: Elizabeth Wright

This book is printed on acid-free, recycled paper.

Visit Chalice Press on the World Wide Web at
www.chalicepress.com

10 9 8 7 6 5 4 3 2 1   99 00 01 02 03

Library of Congress Cataloging–in–Publication Data

Dunnavant, Anthony L. , 1954-
    Founding vocation and future vision : the self-understanding of the Disciples of Christ and the Churches of Christ / by Anthony L. Dunnavant, Richard T. Hughes, Paul M. Blowers.
        p.   cm.
    Includes bibliographical references.
    ISBN 0-8272-1024-8
    1. Restoration movement.   2. Christian Churches (Disciples of Christ).
I. Hughes, Richard T. (Richard Thomas), 1943– . II. Blowers, Paul M.,
1955– . III. Title.
BX7315.D87 1999
286.6'3 — dc21   98-32159
                                                                      CIP
            Printed in the United States of America

This book is dedicated to Forrest F. Reed (1897–1975) on the 100th anniversary of his birth.

Forrest Reed's vision and committed stewardship make possible the Disciples of Christ Historical Society's Reed Lectures. The lectures published in this book were concluded in the centennial month of his birth.

A gift from Katherine M. Reed in conjunction with a gift from the Disciples of Christ Historical Society's James M. and Mary Dudley Seale Publications Fund celebrate his life and witness by underwriting the publication of this volume.

Contents

Preface

Ninety years of separation—how the tone of language has changed. Loud, acerbic, wounding words, after ninety years, have quieted to thoughtful analysis, modest self-assessment, and even appreciative understanding of the other.

In 1906, the formal separation of the Disciples of Christ and Churches of Christ was recognized. In 1995 and 1997, after ninety years, the Disciples of Christ Historical Society invited two distinguished scholars of the separated groups to explore the distinctive perceptions of the founding vision and how that vision has evolved in the two fellowships. This scholarly effort contributes to an important trust adopted by the Disciples of Christ Historical Society. The Society, through the work of a community of historians, fosters understanding, healing, and reconciliation among the branches of the Stone-Campbell movement. Toward that end I offer *Founding Vocation and Future Vision: The Self-understanding of the Disciples of Christ and the Churches of Christ,* the published version of the Historical Society's 1995 and 1997 Reed Lectures.

Anthony L. Dunnavant and Richard T. Hughes are able scholars of irenic spirit. Dr. Dunnavant was professor of church history at Lexington Theological Seminary at the time of his lecture in September 1995. He subsequently has become dean of that Disciples institution. Richard T. Hughes is distinguished professor, Religion Division, Pepperdine University, Malibu, California, a well-known school for the Churches of Christ.

Professor Dunnavant cites the first Reed Lecture, in which Barnett Blakemore identifies the progression of Disciples history "from debate through the concept of discussion to the concept of dialogue." The rhetoric of ninety years ago could be characterized fully as debate, in some instances acrimonious, in others as pained resignation. In these lectures the progression has moved to full expression of discussion. Note, however, that the work goes further. It opens the door to dialogue. Ronald E. Osborn and Paul M. Blowers invite our own dialogue with Professors Dunnavant and Hughes. Ronald Osborn's introduction sets the tone. He is widely celebrated across the Stone-Campbell Movement for careful scholarship graciously offered. He is often credited with identifying freedom as a formative founding value of the movement. Both Hughes and Dunnavant, in dialogue fashion, pick up Osborn's earlier ideas and add to them.

Paul Blowers of Emmanuel School of Religion enters the dialogue as one within the Stone-Campbell Movement. In respect to this conversation, however, his approach is from the distinctive perspective of a deeply interested outsider. He is neither Disciple nor Church of Christ. Yet he is aware and committed to Stone-Campbell history as a teacher in the nondenominational Christian Churches/Churches of Christ. Professor Blowers has considered the lectures and responses given at the time of presentation and has written his own reflections. His essay not only comments on the material but, again in dialogue style, contributes unique information and insight to the conversation.

The full circle of the dialogue, in print, is concluded by comments by the lecturers. The lecturers have the first and last words. "In print" is operative. The dialogue may well continue beyond this book in the thoughts of the readers and, where the reading is done by a community, in their continuing conversation.

The Reed Lectures and this volume are possible only because of the generous support of friends of the Society, friends of Stone-Campbell history. The Valley Church of Van Nuys, California, hosted the 1995 lectures. My predecessor, James M. Seale, gave administrative oversight to the first lectures and recruited Dr. Dunnavant and Dr. Hughes to be lecturers. In addition the James M. and Mary Dudley Seale Publication Fund at the Historical Society helped underwrite the costs of this volume. The administration and faculty of Lipscomb University, Nashville, particularly Richard C. Goode, were gracious hosts for the second lecture. I was pleased that friends from the Churches of Christ made it possible to present President Stephen F. Flatt with a life membership in the Historical Society on that occasion.

I open the door and invite you into Avalon House, the historic residence of David Lipscomb. It is the evening meal before the Reed Lectures at Lipscomb University. Professor Hughes and his wife

Jan are there. Members of the Lipscomb community and the Historical Society Lectures Committee are being seated at tables. But note especially Katherine Reed with friends and members of her family. Katherine is 93 years old and the life of the party.

The meal is a celebration of the centennial of the birth of her husband, Forrest F. Reed. His story is briefly told: reared in Mississippi in an a cappella Church of Christ. An uncle was a primary mentor in the faith. This uncle's own faith had been shaped by experiences in the Civil War, including the walk home across hundreds of miles at the war's end. In later years Forrest became a leader of a Disciples congregation, Woodmont Christian Church of Nashville, and a leading trustee of the Disciples of Christ Historical Society. How appropriate that one who appreciated his life in both fellowships be the patron of these lectures. The tone for dialogue was set as separated brothers and sisters broke bread in the home of one of the saints of the church, David Lipscomb, and remembered Forrest Reed. The ongoing dialogue between us is a fitting tribute to one whose gifts to the world will extend far beyond the century that we celebrated.

Peter M. Morgan, President
Disciples of Christ Historical Society

Introduction

It began with a dream in a lonely wilderness where scattered Christians far from home, weakened by their isolation from one another and the subversion of the inclusive gospel by an undue insistence on the peculiar emphases of the various denominations, suffered the "jarrings and janglings of a party spirit."

Into that scene came dreamers who boldly foresaw an undivided church with Christian believers esteeming one another "as the precious saints of God,… children of the same family and Father, temples of the same Spirit, members of the same body," and workers together in the divine mission of converting the world, living and laboring together in sweet reasonableness after the manner of the original apostolic community, guided now by the New Testament, and uncoerced by any exercise of human dominion, whether expressed through postbiblical creed, official theology, ecclesiastical authority, or other form of arbitrary power.

That dream drew scores of thousands into the movement launched by Barton W. Stone and Thomas and Alexander Campbell. Across the new American West, Christian Churches and Churches of Christ sprang up like flowers in the wilderness, building white meetinghouses at country crossroads or on village corners and erecting structures of stone or brick in the growing urban centers. By the late nineteenth century, Disciples of Christ had begun to celebrate their becoming "a great people."

Not surprisingly, however, earnest believers found themselves attracted by particular elements of the shining vision, some cherishing one element as of supreme and determinative importance, some focusing on another. Varying versions of the dream ("the Plea") resulted, each shaped by a dominant emphasis that cast the other elements as subordinate and in the process refashioned the whole. Accordingly, this movement to unite the divided house of God suffered its own divisions. Formal recognition of the Churches of Christ and the Disciples of Christ as separate bodies appeared in the Federal Religious Census of 1906, publicly advertising the embarrassing reality—which however had been undeniable for some time. In my early ministry, I frequently encountered good people who had lived through that division; some carried the pain and a sense of abandonment in their hearts—and some did not hesitate to express the sentiment, "Good riddance!" Even though a new generation had come on the scene, preachers still held before their hearers the issues disputed in that schism, and congregations experienced virtually no fellowship between the two camps, no exchange of pulpits. Members almost never heard preachers from the separated groups, except in highly promoted revival meetings or at large funerals in small towns. In whatever way the diverse heirs of the founders envisioned the dream, it was not likely to include those who visualized it differently.

By mid-twentieth century, a second division was clearly shaping up. No longer deniable by the late 1960s, it resulted in Christian Churches and Churches of Christ on one hand and the Christian Church (Disciples of Christ) on the other. Again, fellowship between the separated groups was rare; few exchanges of pulpits took place, and little longing was in evidence to restore associations that had once prevailed.

Still the dream would not die. The Reed Lectures that follow in this book give dramatic evidence of a new element in the situation: *the historians of the three groups are talking with one another, listening respectfully, and learning.* This is a new thing. It would be fair to characterize as conscientious chroniclers and unblushing apologists most of those who until recently composed histories of the three groups. We who come after them are in their debt for gathering and preserving much factual material that otherwise would have been lost. Yet their determination to prove to their readers the truth advocated by their particular group is clear. Their target audience was the "true believers" with whom they were affiliated, not the larger community of the total Stone-Campbell movement, much less the historians of American Christianity in general. Today's scholars, by contrast, consult together, and join one another in critical but friendly discussions of their narratives and interpretations. Such interchange has brought about a new appreciation of once vilified controversial figures and a deeper understanding of issues and influences.

While devout believers may be justified in attributing this new climate of openness to the work of the Holy Spirit, the historian (perhaps equally devout) searches for those demonstrable forces in our history that have contributed to this happier situation (and through which the Spirit may be said to have worked). Here it is appropriate to mention three important factors in this development.

First, take note of the Disciples of Christ Historical Society, founded in 1941 to gather, preserve, and make available for use materials relating to the backgrounds and development of "Disciples of Christ, Christian Churches, Churches of Christ, and related groups." That broad intent was the vision of Claude E. Spencer, who began collecting long before the Society came into being and whose insistence on inclusivity, both in collecting and serving, has characterized the Society from its very beginning. For half a century, historians in increasing numbers have sought out the resources of DCHS and have found a ready welcome by its staff, whatever their connection.

Second, take note of the Reed Lectures, which bear the name of a distinguished Nashville church leader and publisher of great vision, energy, and dedication. When Eva Jean Wrather suggested to Forrest F. Reed the possibility of persuading the Historical Society to locate in their city, he became chairman of the committee that brought it there and underwrote its operations for its first few years in Tennessee. One of the chief appeals of DCHS to Mr. Reed, who as a Disciple also had close ties with members of the Churches of Christ, was the inclusiveness of the Society's intention and willingness to serve. The lectureship that he endowed and that bears his name has demonstrated that inclusiveness in the themes addressed and has provided a meeting-place for historians of all three groups. The fascinating and insightful lectures presented in this volume deserve particular attention, setting a new high-water mark in that inclusiveness.

Third, consider the Thomas W. Phillips Memorial, the splendid building that houses the collection and offices of DCHS. Member of a family long distinguished by its generosity to higher education and major benefactors to several colleges of the church, B. D. Phillips was so attracted by the inclusive intention of the Historical Society that he contributed the funds to erect its building as a memorial to his father shortly after the move to Nashville. Here the constantly growing holdings of the Society, carefully catalogued and indexed, annually attract hundreds of visitors, including especially dozens of scholars from all three groups within the

Stone-Campbell Movement, who find here the documents and periodicals they need for their investigations. Intellectual friendships growing out of informal contacts by researchers have sharpened insights, broadened vision, and stimulated the development of fresh interpretations. Particularly important have been the conferences of historians held here to promote interchange of views and insights.

It is pleasing to note concerning the three influences just mentioned that together they represent the three major "streams" of the movement. The Historical Society from its beginning held the status of an "agency," reporting regularly to each successive International Convention of Disciples of Christ and now, as an administrative unit, to each General Assembly of the Christian Church (Disciples of Christ). The Reed Lectureship commemorates a churchman who believed keenly in the importance of solidarity in historical ventures with the Churches of Christ and led the successful effort to bring the Society to Nashville, a major center of their strength. B. D. Phillips, the generous steward who conceived the ideal of the Thomas W. Phillips Memorial to pay honor to his father, found his spiritual home with the Christian Churches and Churches of Christ. Thus, each of the three groups has contributed significantly to the constructive influences being discusssed.

Profoundly affected by the influences just noted, the lectures in this volume represent a new stage in publications dealing with the "movement." For within the covers of this book, established historians from all three groups offer interpretation and comment on the tradition itself and on the task of the scholar who seeks to interpret its past. May all who read find themselves more fully envisioning and more deeply understanding "the dream."

Ronald E. Osborn

CHAPTER 1

Continuities, Changes, and Conflicts

The Founders' Understanding of the Disciples Movement

Anthony L. Dunnavant

Thirty years have passed since the Forrest F. Reed Lectures were established by Mr. Reed's gift, announced in the fall of 1964, and inaugurated in November of 1965.[1] It is noteworthy that the topic of the first Reed Lectures was Disciples of Christ ecclesiology, or understanding of church. The first Reed Lecturer was William Barnett Blakemore.[2]

Dr. Blakemore was dean of the Disciples Divinity House of the University of Chicago and had recently served as the chairman of the Panel of Scholars. This Panel's *Reports*, of which Dean Blakemore was the general editor, were a significant part of the intellectual and theological backdrop of Restructure. Restructure, of course, was the process by which one branch of the Stone-Campbell Movement developed the *Design* by which it constituted itself the Christian Church (Disciples of Christ).

Dean Blakemore not only chaired and edited for the Panel of Scholars but also contributed to its *Reports* some of their most influential contents in terms of their impact on the Restructure process.[3] In addition to this, he served on the Central Committee of the Restructure commission. For these reasons, as well as to commemorate the thirty-year or "generational" anniversary of the Reed Lectures, it is useful to recall the themes of Dean Blakemore's lectures.

The first Reed Lectures were published by Reed and Company for the Disciples of Christ Historical Society in 1966 with the title *The Discovery of the Church* and with the subtitle *A History of Disciple Ecclesiology.* Dean Blakemore's approach in the lectures comprising this volume was to place the development of the Disciples of Christ concept of church in a framework of movement from "debate through the concept of discussion to the concept of dialogue." The field of vision for the lectures was Disciples relationships to the historic churches (especially Disciples' Reformed forebears), to the world, and to Roman Catholicism.[4]

In an intriguing "Forward Look," Blakemore extended his vantage point to include Disciples contact with non-Christian religions and, with greater emphasis, to their relationship with the Christian Orthodoxy rooted in the "Ancient East." He suggested that:

> As the Disciples come more and more into relationship with Orthodoxy, they will increasingly comprehend the eschatological dimensions of the church. The development of this dimension in Disciple consciousness goes on at present only episodically.[5]

Even such a cursory glance at the shape and content of the first Reed Lectures serves to remind us of the context for those lectures. Their historical setting was that they came at the midpoint of the decade of Restructure, and of the Second Vatican Council in the Roman Catholic Church, and of the launching of the Consultation on Church Union. This decade, the 1960s, also became a decade of now legendary tumult and symbolic upheaval in American culture. Such a context brought to the fore, with special urgency for those becoming the Christian Church (Disciples of Christ), questions that had been present throughout the life of the Stone-Campbell Movement:

What is the essential character of the movement? What holds it together, or, more accurately, has failed to? What is its relationship to the wider Christian world, or does such vocabulary even make sense? What is its place in human history under God?

Such questions have not only been perennial ones for the Stone-Campbell Movement in general but have been revisited in this lectureship a number of times. Indeed, the Reed Lectures for 1966 broached the question of *Disciples and The Church Universal* with Robert O. Fife, David Edwin Harrell, Jr., and Ronald E. Osborn representing the three major branches of the Stone-Campbell Movement. Each addressed the questions of "the historic contribution of his group to the church universal and the current status of the group's relationship to the church."[6] As illuminating as it would be in some ways, there will be no further enumeration of the Reed Lectures by topic and speaker. Recalling, however, the trajectory of those earliest ones is a reminder that grappling with those questions of the core character of the Stone-Campbell Movement and of its relationships to the historic churches and to the wider world is the tradition of this lectureship.

In keeping with Dean Blakemore's image of thirty years ago, the aim here is to engage in discussion, at the very least, if not dialogue. That is, the assumption is that "theological origins" may be found in the early days of the Stone-Campbell heritage for each of the current branches of the movement.

My purpose, as a speaker standing within the Christian Church (Disciples of Christ) is not to claim that it is the true, only, or even best contemporary expression of our theological heritage. Rather, it is to highlight those elements in the movement's early self-understanding that are discernible as trajectories toward the peculiar emphases or character of the present-day Christian Church (Disciples of Christ).

My focus in both lectures will be on Disciples of Christ self-understanding primarily as it relates to mission and structure beyond the local congregation and in relation to the church and the world outside our movement. This is because the affirmation that our *congregations* are "church" has been made across the spectrum of our movement, has never been controversial, and, therefore, is not part of the "roots of division."

Further, my purpose will be to account for the *distinctive responses* to changing contexts that became formative for what was to become the Christian Church (Disciples of Christ). My references to the founders, especially to the Campbells, will be less a reconstruction (even in summary form) of their overall thought than a window onto the features of their thought that one branch of the movement has seen fit to cherish in memory.

Our thinking about differing responses to circumstances might be informed by the use of a couple of images. We might think of the church's experience in history as being analogous to whitewater rafting. When rocks or other obstacles, including other rafts, appear in the rapidly moving stream, the "rafters" have to choose quickly to steer one way or the other to avoid collision. The "raft" that became the Christian Church (Disciples of Christ) steered one way at several junctures that placed it on a different trajectory than that of what became the Churches of Christ and, later, the undenominational fellowship of Christian Churches and Churches of Christ.

Another image we might use is that of a downhill skier, who also leans one way or another to avoid obstacles. The direction of the "lean," however, does more than avoid the obstacle. It also shapes the subsequent path of descent. (Alexander Campbell was, himself, aware of the influence of "leaning." He remarked of himself that: "I was once so straight, that, like the Indian's tree, I leaned a little the other way.")[7]

Thesis

The thesis of this lecture is that the vector[8] within the Stone-Campbell Movement that leads to the Christian Church (Disciples of Christ) is one that seeks to hold together versions of the movement's shared commitments to freedom, apostolicity, unity, and evangelism with an ethos of catholicity that is congruent with a "providential worldview."

Much of the task here will be to illustrate the presence of that providential worldview and point to some instances in which the ethos of catholicity was called forth. Before turning to that, however, some explanation may be in order for the phrase "the movement's shared commitments to freedom, apostolicity, unity, and evangelism." What follows is my own appropriation of mid-to-late twentieth-century Disciples of Christ historical interpretation of the Stone-Campbell Movement. Since this took place in Christian Church (Disciples of Christ) circles, it may be taken as illustrative and probably not atypical.

In Christian Church (Disciples of Christ) circles, there is broad familiarity among scholars, pastors, and students of our history with the most conventional tradition of interpretation of the Stone-Campbell Movement. That is, that it may be identified as a movement that sought the unity (or the reunion) of the Church on the basis of the restoration of the apostolic faith and order. The unity-and-restoration approach to interpretation has been used to point to some key dimensions of the movement's life. It has been used to describe some of the dynamics that have divided it. That is, there

is considerable insight in the view that the movement has historically polarized into restoration camps and unity camps.

These two emphases (unity and restoration) have certainly been
key ones. Nevertheless, these two ideals have sometimes been taken
out of context and treated as if they represented the sole identifying commitments of the Disciples. Contrary to this most dominant
broad perspective for generations, at least as early as W. T. Moore
in 1909, a number of interpreters have reminded us that the Stone-
Campbell Movement was also profoundly committed to freedom.[9]

The Forrest F. Reed Lectures by Ronald E. Osborn in our
nation's bicentennial year, later published as *Experiment in Liberty*,
both argued for and helped to establish in Christian Church (Disciples of Christ) consciousness the notion that we were an ecclesiastical freedom movement as well as a restoration movement and
a unity movement.[10]

Building in part on Professor Osborn's work, the most recent
(as of 1995) historical overview of the Disciples of Christ to be published by the denomination's publishing house begins with a three-
principle approach to our history before turning to the themes of
sacraments, mission, and ecclesiology. In the first edition of *Joined
in Discipleship* Mark Toulouse writes of the interpretation principle,
the restoration principle, and the ecumenical principle. Much of
his discussion of the interpretation principle relates to the concept
of freedom.[11]

With this as background, my own work in Disciples of Christ
history has focused on historiography, theological ideology, and
the development of polity. What I have emphasized is the
movement's commitment to the vision of Jesus' prayer as found in
John 17:20–23:

> I do not pray for these only, but also for those who believe
> in me through their word, that they may all be one; even
> as thou, Father, art in me, and I in thee, that they also may
> be in us, so that the world may believe that thou has sent
> me. The glory which thou hast given me I have given to
> them, that they may be one even as we are one, I in them
> and thou in me, that they may become perfectly one, so
> that the world may know that thou hast sent me and hast
> loved them even as thou has loved me. (RSV)

Rooting the Stone-Campbell Movement's development in its
preoccupation with the vision of this text has placed me, sometimes quite unconsciously, in the interpretive tradition of such

writers as Hiram Van Kirk and, more recently, Dean E. Walker, among others. Van Kirk, in his 1907 work *The Rise of the Current Reformation*, put it this way:

> Like the Protestant Reformation which went before and furnished both motive and model for its successor, the Current Reformation was carried out on definite principles...These principles are threefold:—
>
> 1. Conversion of the World.
> 2. Union of All Christians.
> 3. Restoration of Primitive Christianity.
>
> These principles constituted the aim of the Current Reformation and are the basis of the Plea of the Disciples of Christ, and around them may be written the history of this interesting people. They were worked out in a long and painful process in conflict with the religious establishments of the time. They found Biblical sanction in the final prayer of Jesus, and are worthy of our consideration in every way as the statement of a high-minded programme.

Van Kirk goes on to state that "the Conversion of the World is the ultimate principle," "the Union of Christians is the *material principle*," and "the Restoration of Primitive Christianity is the *formal* principle."[12] To put the same point another way, the *tactics* of Christian primitivism were seen as the specific *strategy* for Christian unity, in pursuit of the objective of the evangelization of the world.[13]

Adding to Van Kirk's threefold scheme the consciousness of freedom as both a powerful contextual factor and an internal dimension of Disciples life (as Ronald Osborn reminded us), I believe that a useful summation of the Disciples plea might be as follows:

> Grateful for the freedom given in the Providence of God to the United States, Disciples sought to respond faithfully by identifying and embodying the apostolic basis for the unity and reform of the Church. They were convinced that only a Church so reformed and so unified on this apostolic and catholic basis could convince the world of human beings of the truth of the Gospel. A world of persons so convinced and, thereby, converted to Christ would be

transformed, social ills ameliorated, and the way prepared for the coming millennium.

I am prepared to admit, reluctantly, that the foregoing formulation is slightly more cumbersome than "unity-through-restoration." It seems to me, however, to be a version of the Stone-Campbell "plea" that accounts for the particular development of the Christian Church (Disciples of Christ). Note especially what may be the less familiar nuances in it: alongside unity-through-restoration are the emphases on divine providence; evangelization as the persuasion to the truth, as inculcation of personal discipleship, and as social amelioration; and the context of Christian eschatological hope.

We shall take up issues related to the changing definitions of mission and evangelism in the next lecture, for this was a driving force behind structural development among the Disciples of Christ. But here we pause to ask if there were something present early in the movement that positions or prepares one stream of it to develop those particular mission concepts and structures?

This question brings us back to our thesis and may be answered, at least in part, by giving attention to what David Edwin Harrell, Jr., called the "millennialistic and providential world view of the Disciples of Christ."[14] Robert Frederick West a generation earlier, Harrell himself, and more recently a growing list of colleagues have called attention to the specifically "millennialistic," side of this worldview but it is its overarching "providential" character that will receive our attention.[15] This basic outlook is one of the important continuities in the early history of the movement as seen from the Christian Church (Disciples of Christ) perspective.

To illustrate that this perspective is a *continuity* in early Disciples life, the focus will be primarily on Thomas and Alexander Campbell. Walter Scott will be mentioned to provide both confirmation and some contrast. That is, Scott also illustrates at least one conflict in the movement's self-understanding. Barton W. Stone will be discussed in the next lecture because his impact on the Christian Church (Disciples of Christ) may be more important as twentieth-century appropriation than nineteenth-century trajectory. (That is, I accept and assume the basic conclusions of Richard Hughes's and C. Leonard Allen's theses about the "apocalyptic origins" of the Churches of Christ and of Stone's nineteenth-century impact on that part of our movement.)

Alexander Campbell was neither being innovative nor expressing any late development in his thought, when he noted in 1853 that "Divine providence extends, not merely to every sphere, but to every atom of every sphere in the whole universe."[16] Both Robert Richardson and Selina Huntington Campbell report that Mr. Campbell was not only a believer in the kind of general or ordinary providence just alluded to, but also in extraordinary or "special providences."[17] Mrs. Campbell recalled that she had

> heard Mr. Campbell remark, 'that nothing of importance even happened to him through life, without some indication or premonition being given to him.' He was not superstitious, but he was a great believer in special Providences. Would it not be very strange were it otherwise, seeing he had so many instances of the interposition of a kind, unseen hand through his whole journey?[18]

By the time of his 1853 observation on providence, Alexander Campbell's adult thought and church leadership had undergone many changes. Certainly the tone and emphases of his editorial leadership and the character and range of his churchly and educational roles were quite different from those of forty or even twenty-five years earlier. Eva Jean Wrather set some of these changes forth helpfully in her *Creative Freedom in Action* as she traces Mr. Campbell from iconoclast to advocate of organization. Further, by the 1850s Alexander Campbell was well on the way in terms of his "Millennial Odyssey" from "primitive church to Protestant nation" and finally to primitive Christian faith.[19] But beyond changes in editorial tone, in leadership emphasis, or even in the presumed favored instrument of millennial fulfillment there is continuity in the assumption of God's active providence. And this continuity extends to the earliest days of the movement.

Note the presence of a providential framework in some passages from the 1809 "Declaration and Address of the Christian Association of Washington, Pennsylvania." In this most influential founding document of our Stone-Campbell tradition, Thomas Campbell looks at recent history to discern the providence of God:

> The auspicious phenomena of the times furnish collateral arguments of a very encouraging nature, that our dutiful and pious endeavors shall not be in vain in the Lord…Have not greater efforts been made, and more done, for the

promulgation of the Gospel among the nations, since the commencement of the French Revolution, than had been for many centuries prior to that event? And have not the Churches, both in Europe and America, since that period discovered a more than usual concern for the removal of contentions, for the healing of divisions…Should *we* not, then, be excited by these considerations to concur with all our might, to help forward this good work; that what yet remains to be done, may be fully accomplished.[20]

Here Thomas Campbell's focus is on "efforts" on behalf of the Gospel and on the "concern" of the Churches as he looked for the purposes of God beneath the unfolding of certain "good work" in "Europe and America." Father Campbell's discerning view of these efforts, this concern, and this work, was immediately pressed into the service of extending a call to "concur" and to "help" in it. Discernment was linked to vocation and, conversely, vocation defined with reference to something larger than one's own activity.

This linkage of discernment to vocation is not limited to a narrow focus on religious or purely church-based factors in history. The "Declaration and Address," also, in a passage directed especially to "gospel ministers," sees providential meaning in the political arrangements of the young United States. First it declares its discernment that the historical context is:

The favorable opportunity which Divine Providence has put into your hands, in this happy country, for the accomplishment of so great a good, is, in itself, a consideration of no small encouragement. A country happily exempted from the baneful influence of a civil establishment of any peculiar form of Christianity;

Then it moves to the issue of vocation, of providential calling:

…Still more happy will it be for us if we duly esteem and improve those great advantages, for the high and valuable ends for which they are manifestly given, and sure where much is given, much also will be required. Can the Lord expect, or require, anything less from a people in such unhampered circumstances—from a people so liberally furnished with all means and mercies, than a thorough reformation in all things, civil and religious, according to

This passage names as well as any the context for the birth of the Campbell side of our heritage—the religious freedom of the United States of America providentially interpreted and powerfully linked to vocation. Some of you with sharp ears and long memories will recall this passage from Thomas Campbell having been quoted in another Reed Lecture, that by Ronald E. Osborn in 1976. Indeed, "Thomas Campbell's Manifesto" does, as Professor Osborn showed, illustrate that our founders were "champions of freedom" who launched an "experiment in liberty."[22]

Dr. Osborn's statement that best captured our forebears' reading of their times, however, is that they believed that "their situation in the young nation provided a heaven-sent opportunity for starting anew."[23] That "heaven-sent opportunities" called for response, called for "starting anew," again reminds us of the relationship between providence and vocation.

Alexander Campbell illustrates the relationship between providence and vocation in the way he entered into Christian ministry. Robert Richardson describes Alexander Campbell's Christmas Day 1811 review of the "Divine guidings and the providential dispensations he had experienced" relative to his ordination. There are listed from Campbell twelve "special instances of Divine power which I consider to bind me under obligations to be specially devoted to Him, with my whole mind, soul and body." That the correct category is "providence" is signalled by the phrase "instances of Divine power." What follows is a blend of quite "ordinary" facts of parentage, marriage, circumstances, interest, talents, and temperament with claims of "extraordinary deliverance" "when at imminent danger at sea" and the observation that his education was "providential in the following respects:

> 1. In my grand design being, not to preach the Gospel, but to shine in literary honors and affluence. 2. In my design being frustrated, and my mind turned to desire that office. 3. In my being introduced, quite contrary to expectation, to the University of Glasgow, and the literary advantages there."[24]

The prominence in Alexander Campbell's thought of an overarching view of humanity's history under God with its successive dispensations is a point that needs to be remembered but need not be belabored here.[25] What is more relevant to our case is that Alexander Campbell's early acknowledgment that providence could lead one in directions "quite contrary to expectation" was echoed in later expressions of humility relative to human knowledge and certainty.

Campbell began his *Christian System* with the topic "The Universe" and in this passage noted that the parts of anything could never be known apart from the whole, the whole never known apart from its ultimate design, and that design never fully known "without a perfect intelligence of that *incomprehensible* Being by whom and for whom all things were created and made" (emphasis added, note the ironic juxtaposition—one needs "a perfect intelligence" of an "incomprehensible Being"). Therefore, he notes:

> How gracefully, then, sits unassuming modesty on all the reasonings of man! The true philosopher and the true Christian, therefore, delight always to appear in the unaffected costume of humility, candor, and docility.[26]

The viewpoint that saw things, including their own lives and ministries, in the light of larger realities was shared by Thomas and Alexander Campbell and represents one of the significant continuities in the early self-understanding of the movement. Almost a quarter-century after the publication of the "Declaration and Address," Alexander Campbell wrote an article on "Disciples of Christ" for Fessenden and Co.'s *Encyclopedia of Religious Knowledge*. In this article Campbell notes that at "about the commencement of the present century, the Bible alone, without any human addition in the form of creeds or confessions of faith, began to be pled and preached by many distinguished ministers of different denominations, both in Europe and America."

Campbell certainly goes on to describe the distinctiveness of the Disciples of Christ in history, doctrine, and practice, but he had first placed the Disciples in relation to a wider reality. Furthermore, he noted that the Disciples' division with the Baptist association had been "by constraint, not of choice" from the Disciples' perspective.[27]

A similar, at least partially appreciative, description of historical background (especially of Luther's reform) appears in the 1835 preface to *The Christian System*. Although emphasis is again placed on the uniqueness of the Campbells' own movement, and in terms that would embarrass many contemporary Disciples, there is nonetheless a breadth of view.[28] There is a degree of ambiguity here: between the *fact* of this broader view and the *way* the Campbells placed themselves in wider histories. In the consciousness of the Christian Church (Disciples of Christ), however, the tendency of the founders to see themselves within a larger framework, their efforts to unite or to remain in union with other Christians, and their own statements with regard to what they called "sectarianism" become grounds for resolving the ambiguity in a direction expressive of a catholic spirit.

It is recalled with emphasis in such Christian Church (Disciples of Christ) accounts of the Stone-Campbell story as McAllister and Tucker's *Journey in Faith* that the Campbells sought relationship with the Presbyterian Synod of Pittsburgh in 1810, began exploring association with the Baptists in 1812, joined the Redstone Association by 1815, gradually separated from the Baptists by about 1830, and almost immediately began the process of union with the Stoneite Christians.[29] In short, the impulse toward relationship with other Christians in the founding generation is well remembered among us.

Through the work of historians such as David Thompson and Hiram Lester, Thomas Campbell is remembered as having participated in the interdenominational Evangelical Society of Ulster.[30] We also remember that Father Campbell's famous 1809 "Declaration" included the address: "to all that love our Lord Jesus Christ, in sincerity, throughout all the Churches."[31] The impulse to relate with and to the wider Christian world seems present here.

Walter Scott, the evangelist, close associate of the Campbells, and conventionally defined member of the "four founders," provides some confirmation for the notion that the Campbells were sensitive to the ambiguity of their particularity in the pursuit of unity and vigilant about not resolving that in a presumptuous, too self-congratulatory way. Scott included in the preface to his 1836 *The Gospel Restored* the by-now-familiar sort of contextual observation that:

> The professors of our holy religion having unhappily strayed from the scriptures and true Christianity, there seemed to be no remedy in any thing but a return to original ground. This suggested itself to many, in different places, almost simultaneously, about the beginning of the present century, and numerous churches were formed about that time, both in Europe and America, resembling, more or less, the churches planted by the Apostles, or the church of Jerusalem instituted by the Lord Jesus Himself.

So far this is familiar. It sounds just like Thomas Campbell in the "Declaration and Address" or Alexander Campbell in his encyclopedia article; Scott is simply setting the stage of the general providential ground for his movement's particular efforts. But he goes on to remark later that:

> The present century, then, is characterized by these three successive steps, which the lovers of our Lord Jesus have been enabled to make, in their return to the original institution. First the Bible was adopted as sole authority in our assemblies, to the exclusion of all other books. Next the Apostolic order was proposed. Finally the True Gospel was restored.[32]

This sounds pretty cut-and-dried. The ambiguity of particularity within a wider history seems resolved in the direction of the claim of fait accompli. Is this view in conflict with Campbell's assertion of the uniqueness of their restoration efforts? Alexander Campbell seemed to think so. His response is renowned: "I cannot regard anything done by him in 1827, or myself in 1823, as a restoration of the Gospel of Christ either to the church or to the world."[33] To Campbell, Scott's claim went too far.

Campbell's negative response to Scott's bold claim may well have had several roots.[34] My inference is that Campbell's (at least formal) humility or catholicity of spirit was at least one of the roots of his negative response to Scott. This exchange points to a significant attitudinal divergence within the movement.

I am very conscious that I have used the term "catholic" without defining it yet in this context. I mean it in the classical sense of "general" and "universal." It implies a broad outlook that judges parts in relationship to the whole, and, therefore, it approaches being synonymous with our current term "holistic."

It is an especially good word to apply to this ethos or attitude as it relates to the Campbells' judgments about the boundaries of Christian fellowship and Christian identity, because they looked for Christianity in the totality, the whole, of persons' lives.

As a description of an attitude present (or at least striven for!) but not necessarily dominant in the Stone-Campbell Movement, "catholic ethos" refers to something other than being opposed to the church's being divided into denominations. This kind of "catholicity" or "antidenominationalism" was, of course, shared in principle by the whole movement so that to say that a vector in the movement held its common ideals in a "catholic" way would seem to be redundant.

Rather, there is something *more* than the movement's common, formal, "antidenominationalism" that occasionally appeared in the founders' utterance that helps set a trajectory. It is an attitude that is more easily illustrated than defined. I believe it is sustained by a broad and providential worldview, closely akin to humility, and that it underlies what follows. The quotation is from Alexander Campbell. It came in response to a letter from "An Independent Baptist" dated February 11, 1826. (This is a text that both Prof. Richard Hughes and Eva Jean Wrather have called to our attention in different contexts.) The letter-writer had criticized Mr. Campbell for claiming to be in "full communion" with Baptists and yet freely publishing his disagreements with them. Mr. Campbell replies:

> Dear sir, this plan of making our own nest, and fluttering over our own brood; of building our own tent, and of confining all goodness and grace to our noble selves and the "elect few" who are like us, is the quintessence of sublimated pharisaism. The old Pharisees were but babes in comparison to the modern; and the longer I live, and the more I reflect upon God and man—heaven and earth— the Bible and the world—the Redeemer and his church— the more I am assured that all sectarianism is the offspring of hell…

In nineteenth-century parlance such as this "pharisaism" was meant to convey pride, narrowness of relationship and self-righteousness. We needn't endorse Campbell's view of the first-century Pharisees in order to take his point relative to nineteenth-century sectarianism. It is noteworthy that Campbell locates his viewpoint on this issue in relation to reflection on the larger scheme of things: God and humanity, heaven and earth, the Bible and the world, Christ and the church. Campbell concludes the paragraph by saying:

> To lock ourselves up in the bandbox of our own little circle; to associate with a few units, tens, or hundreds, as the pure church, as the elect, is real Protestant monkery, it is evangelical pharisaism.[35]

Alexander Campbell's position here would be seen in Christian Church (Disciples of Christ) circles as harking back to that of the "Declaration and Address" and anticipating that of the "Lunenburg" correspondence. Elsewhere in the letter "To an Independent Baptist," Campbell had noted his correspondent's definition of "full communion" as "full union in the common worship, doctrines, and institutions of any church or denomination." He replied that under such a definition of "full communion," he did "not think the Savior himself could have instituted the supper amongst the twelve."[36]

In contrast to his correspondent's definition Campbell proposes the familiar ground of Christian fellowship: "so long as he confesses with his lips that he believes in his heart this truth [that Jesus is the Christ] and lives conformably to it and supports an unblemished moral character, so long he is a worthy brother."[37] This statement echoes the language of the "Declaration and Address":

> That the Church of Christ upon earth is essentially, intentionally, and constitutionally one; consisting of all those in every place that profess their faith in Christ and obedience to him in all things according to the Scriptures and that manifest the same by their tempers and conduct, and of none else; as none else can be truly and properly called Christians.[38]

Of course, between the 1809 "Declaration and Address" and the 1826 letter, baptism had taken on a unique place in the Campbell movement relative to the practical definition of "obedience to [Christ] in all things according to the Scriptures." This was an important change. But the principle remained that what is practically determinative of Christian identity and the basis for fellowship is one's confession of Jesus Christ and overall manifestation of Christ's lordship in "tempers and conduct." This latter phrase we would call "attitudes and actions" and mean the totality of one's life.

This principle remained to be revisited by Alexander Campbell's 1826 statement that "I frankly own, that my full conviction is, that there are many Paido-Baptist congregations, of whose Christianity, or of whose profession of Christianity, I think as highly as of most Baptist congregations."[39] Since this statement comes in the same document as his stinging denunciation of sectarianism, I am unwilling to read it as a coy slap at the Baptists.

Alexander Campbell's 1837 reply to the Lunenburg correspondent is so well known that I shall not quote it at length here. The principle from it that has been operative in Christian Church (Disciples of Christ) memory is succinctly stated in Mr. Campbell's own language. "I cannot, therefore, make any one duty the standard of Christian state, or character, not even immersion into the name of the Father, of the Son, and of the Holy Spirit, and in my heart regard all those that have been sprinkled in infancy without their knowledge and consent, as aliens from Christ and the well-grounded hope of heaven."[40]

It is understood, at least among some in the Christian Church (Disciples of Christ), that these statements of Thomas and Alexander Campbell did not emerge in a vacuum and that there are many other texts in our tradition that would suggest a deep and firm commitment to both immersion and many other particulars of the "Ancient Order of Things." The prominence of such statements, especially that of the Lunenburg correspondence, in one branch's historical memory does help to name a theological root of the Christian Church (Disciples of Christ).

Between 1809 and 1837, between the "Declaration and Address" and the Lunenburg correspondence, there were many changes in the founders' circumstances, their church relationships, and even in some important features of their particular reading of the religious meaning of their history. In spite of changes, however, there was a continuing providential outlook—a sense of seeking a vision for their vocation: a discernment of what God was doing in their world and among Christians and, thereby, at least partially calling them to do. The most stable, continually revisited ground for understanding their vocation in changing times was the confession of faith in Jesus Christ and submission to his lordship, as they understood it.

These were two foci kept in view: a provident God at work in the world, and Jesus Christ who is that God's Son. These were the foci when new "rocks" arose in the rushing waters of historical changes—changes in context and in worldview. It is perhaps not at all surprising that for the stream of the movement that became the Christian Church (Disciples of Christ), "missions" or "world outreach" on the one hand and "brotherhood" or being Disciples of Christ on the other are the terms that most nearly capture our twentieth-century way of being church.

NOTES

[1]"The Forrest F. Reed Lectureship Established," *Discipliana* 24:5 (November 1964), 59.

[2]"W. B. Blakemore to Give Reed Lectures," *Discipliana* 25:1 (March 1965), 3.

[3]Ibid., See W. B. Blakemore, gen. ed., *The Renewal of Church: The Panel of Scholars Reports*, vol. 1: *The Reformation of Tradition*, ed. Ronald E. Osborn; vol. 2: *The Reconstruction of Theology*, ed. Ralph G. Wilburn; vol. 3: *The Revival of the Churches*, ed. W. B. Blakemore; 3 vols. (St. Louis: Bethany Press, 1963). The specific contributions were "Reasonable, Empirical, Pragmatic: The Mind of Disciples of Christ," 1:161–83; "The Sociology of Disciples Intellectual Life: Historical Forms of Organization for Thinking," 1:257–64; "Where Thought and Action Meet," 3:15–24; "The Issue of Polity for Disciples Today," 3:52–81; "The Christian Task and the Church's Ministry," 3:150–88; and "Worship and the Lord's Supper," 3:227–50.

[4]William Barnett Blakemore, *The Discovery of the Church: A History of Disciples Ecclesiology*, The Reed Lectures for 1965 (Nashville: Reed and Company, 1966). See chapters "Dialogue With the Reformers," 9–35; "Dialogue with the World," 36–63; and "Dialogue with Rome," 64–95.

[5]Ibid., 96–97.

[6]Willis R. Jones, foreword to *Disciples and The Church Universal*, by Robert O. Fife, David Edwin Harrell, Jr., and Ronald E. Osborn, The Reed Lectures for 1966 (Nashville: Disciples of Christ Historical Society, 1967), [7]

[7]Editor [Alexander Campbell], "To an Independent Baptist," *The Christian Baptist* 3 (1825–26); reprint edition; Cincinnati: Printed by J. A. James for D. S. Burnet, 1835 (page references are to the reprint edition), 238.

[8]Here I am using the term "vector" in basically the way suggested by Samuel S. Hill, as a "geometric icon" for an historical phenomenon. The vector "icon" suggests the movement of energy in a certain direction (see Hill, "Cane Ridge Had a Context," in *Cane Ridge in Context: Perspectives on Barton W. Stone and the Revival*, ed. Anthony L. Dunnavant [Nashville: Disciples of Christ Historical Society, 1992], 127).

[9]William T. Moore, *A Comprehensive History of the Disciples of Christ* (New York: Fleming H. Revell Co., 1909).

[10]Ronald E. Osborn, *Experiment in Liberty: The Ideal of Freedom in the Experience of the Disciples of Christ*, The Forrest F. Reed Lectures for 1976 (St. Louis: Bethany Press, 1978).

[11]Mark G. Toulouse, *Joined in Discipleship: the Maturing of an American Religious Movement*, with a foreword by Martin E. Marty (St. Louis: Chalice Press, 1992), 15–16 n. 13, 17–38.

[12]Hiram Van Kirk, *The Rise of the Current Reformation* (St. Louis: Christian Publishing Company, 1907), 109–14.

[13]This language is from my "Evangelization and Eschatology: Lost Link in the Disciples Tradition?" *Lexington Theological Quarterly* 28:1(Spring 1993), 43–54. This essay also contains a more detailed and documented version of these observations on the recent history of historical self-interpretation in the Christian Church (Disciples of Christ).

[14]David Edwin Harrell, Jr., *A Social History of the Disciples of Christ*, vol. 1: *Quest for a Christian America: The Disciples of Christ and American Society to 1866* (Nashville: Disciples of Christ Historical Society, 1966); vol. 2: *The Social Sources of Division in the Disciples of Christ, 1865 to 1900* (Atlanta: Publishing Systems, 1973); 2 vols., 1:46.

[15]Ibid., 44–61; Robert Frederick West, *Alexander Campbell and Natural Religion*, Yale Studies in Religious Education, no. 21 (New Haven: Yale University Press, 1948), 163–217; among the more recent writers on Campbell's and Stone's millennialism are Richard T. Hughes and C. Leonard Allen, *Illusions of Innocence: Protestant Primitivism in America, 1630–1875*, with a foreword by Robert N. Bellah (Chicago and London: University of Chicago Press, 1988), 121–22, 170–87; Hughes, "The Apocalyptic Origins of Churches of Christ," *Religion and American Life: A Jour-

nal of Interpretation 2:2 (Summer 1992), 181–214; Allen, "'The Stone that the Builders Rejected': Barton W. Stone in the Memory of Churches of Christ," in *Cane Ridge in Context: Perspectives on Barton W. Stone and the Revival*, ed. Anthony L. Dunnavant (Nashville: Disciples of Christ Historical Society, 1992), 43–62; Stephen V. Sprinkle, "Alexander Campbell and the Doctrine of the Church," *Discipliana* 48:2 (Summer 1988), 19–25; Hiram J. Lester, "Alexander Campbell's Millennial Program," *Discipliana* 48:3 (Fall 1988), 35–39; Tim Crowley, "A Chronological Delineation of Alexander Campbell's Eschatological Theory from 1823 to 1851," *Discipliana* 54:4 (Winter 1994), 99–107. See also the new chapter on "The Eschatological Principle: God with Us" in Mark G. Toulouse, *Joined in Discipleship: The Shaping of Contemporary Disciples Identity*, revised and expanded ed. (St. Louis: Chalice Press, 1997), 101–35. The term "providence" has all but dropped out of our ordinary vocabulary and would strike many ears as simply quaint now. Perhaps this is less so in the other branches of our movement than in my own, but Bob Barnhill suggested in a 1975 sermon called "The Unseen Hand" that silence largely prevailed on this issue among Churches of Christ as well. C. Leonard Allen's inclusion of a chapter on providence in *Distant Voices: Discovering a Forgotten Past for a Changing Church* (Abilene, Tex.: ACU Press, 1993) implies that the concept may not have much currency among his intended readers. Jack Cottrell's large 1984 volume on the subject of providence for College Press (Joplin, Mo.), entitled *What the Bible Says About God the Ruler*, is itself a recent treatment within the Stone-Campbell orbit of the general theological and biblical topic of providence. The author's focus, however, is not upon the subject of providence as understood in the Stone-Campbell tradition and references within it to that particular heritage are relatively few.

[16]Alexander Campbell, *Millennial Harbinger* 1853, 289–90 quoted in Royal Humbert, ed. *A Compend of Alexander Campbell's Theology: with commentary in the form of critical and historical footnotes* (St. Louis: Bethany Press, 1961), 80.

[17]For Alexander Campbell's reported beliefs, see especially Robert Richardson, *Memoirs of Alexander Campbell: Embracing a View of the Origins, Progress, and Principles of the Religious Reformation which He Advocated* (Philadelphia: J. B. Lippincott & Co., 1868; reprint, Indianapolis: Religious Book Service, n.d. [page references are to the reprint edition]), 1:380–81; also, Selina Huntington Campbell, *Home Life and Reminiscences of Alexander Campbell, By His Wife* (St. Louis: John Burns, Publisher, 1882), 293.

[18]Ibid.

[19]Eva Jean Wrather, *Creative Freedom in Action: Alexander Campbell on the Structure of the Church* (St. Louis: Bethany Press, 1968); Allen and Hughes, *Illusions of Innocence*, 171ff.

[20]*Declaration and Address by Thomas Campbell; Last Will and Testament of the Springfield Presbytery by Barton W. Stone and Others*, with a brief introduction by F. D. Kershner (St. Louis: Bethany Press, 1960), 31.

[21]Ibid., 30–31.

[22]Osborn, *Experiment in Liberty*, 23–24.

[23]Ibid., 24.

[24]Richardson, *Memoirs of Alexander Campbell*, 1:379–81.

[25]On Alexander Campbell's theology as it relates to covenant theology, see Van Kirk, *The Rise of the Current Reformation*.

[26]Alexander Campbell, *The Christian System* (Bethany, Va: By the author, 1839; reprint edition, Nashville: Gospel Advocate Company, 1964), 2.

[27]Alexander Campbell, *The Disciples of Christ*, with a bibliographical introduction by Roscoe M. Pierson, Reprints of Disciple Documents, no. 1 (Lexington: Bosworth Memorial Library, The College of the Bible), 6–11.

[28]A. Campbell, *Christian System*, vii–xv.

[29]Lester G. McAllister and William E. Tucker, *Journey in Faith: A History of the Christian Church (Disciples of Christ)* (St. Louis: Bethany Press, 1975), 115–55.

[30]See, e.g., David M. Thompson, "The Irish Background to Thomas Campbell's

Declaration and Address," *Discipliana* 46 (Summer 1986), 23–27; Hiram J. Lester, "The Case Against Sectarianism," *The Disciple* 17 (March 1990), 10–12.

³¹*Declaration and Address*, 27.

³²Walter Scott, *The Gospel Restored: A Discourse* (Cincinnati: O. H. Donogh, 1836; reprint edition, Joplin, Mo.: College Press, 1986 [page references are to the reprint edition]), v.

³³A.[lexander] Campbell, "Letters from Brother Campbell and Brother Scott," *Evangelist* 7 (November 1839), 259.

³⁴See brief discussion of this episode in Hughes and Allen, *Illusions of Innocence*, 123–25.

³⁵Campbell, "To an Independent Baptist," 238.

³⁶Ibid., 237.

³⁷Ibid.

³⁸*Declaration and Address*, 44.

³⁹"To an Independent Baptist," 238.

⁴⁰A.[lexander] C.[ampbell], "Any Christians Among Protestant Parties." *Millennial Harbinger* September 1837; reprinted in Alexander Campbell, *The Lunenburg Letter with Attendant Comments*, Footnotes to Disciple History, no. 2 (Nashville: Disciples of Christ Historical Society, 1955).

.

CHAPTER 2

Christ and Covenant

Historical Concepts Underlying the Restructured Church

Anthony L. Dunnavant

I have suggested that the theological trajectory or vector out of the founding generation that culminated in the Christian Church (Disciples of Christ) was the desire to contend for the Stone-Campbell movement's distinctive "Plea" while maintaining a catholic or holistic ethos. This trajectory was described as being congruent with, or as arising out of, a providential worldview. Several instances in which this providential perspective was made explicit by the founders were recalled. It was observed that there was a strong linkage between providence and vocation.

Additionally, examples of a catholic ethos were cited that related directly to the issue of Christian identity and fellowship. In these examples, Thomas and Alexander Campbell argued for a catholic/holistic definition of Christian identity based on the confession of Christ and the general manifestation of a Christian life, over against any single act of obedience, even extending this preference for the "whole life" to the "single act" to the act of immersion.

It was noted in passing that this catholic ethos is distinguishable from the overall "antidenominationalism" of the Stone-

Campbell Movement. That is, it was acknowledged that the movement's impulse to embrace providentially given freedom, for the reform and union of the church, on the platform of the apostle's teaching, so that the world might be converted, was understood as, itself, a catholic program.

Specifically, the "Ancient Order of Things," the apostles' teaching, was presented as a catholic platform that included baptism with its ancient, apostolic mode and design. The promotion of the "Plea" was the most usual, normal, and frequent form of catholicity in the early movement.

The meaning of the letter "To an Independent Baptist" and of the Lunenburg correspondence is *not* that these letters represent the most frequent or most nearly typical form of assault on divisions in the body of Christ to issue from Campbell. Rather, they illustrate that, *beyond* the more familiar form of the movement's "antidenominationalism," there was this infrequent, arguably slight, perhaps reluctant, and yet still self-critical refusal to be absolutist.

Why do I characterize it so cautiously? Because only by acknowledging how committed Alexander Campbell *was* to the "Ancient Order" and how persuasive he understood it to be, can we begin to catch the significance of these exceptional statements. Campbell's "usual" sentiments are well caught up in this paragraph from the first entry in his series of articles on "A Restoration of the Ancient Order of Things":

> To bring the societies of christians up to the New Testament, is just to bring the disciples individually and collectively, to walk in the faith, and in the commandments of the Lord and Saviour, as presented in that blessed volume; and this is to restore the ancient order of things.[1]

In Campbell's thought, "the testimony of the apostles" had been anticipated and defined in the intercessory prayer of Jesus (John 17) as the basis of the unity of the church. Alexander Campbell's own succinct statement of the "Plea" is hard to improve upon: "The word of the Apostles, the unity of those who believe it, and the conviction of the world are here inseparably related."[2]

To Campbell "the word of the Apostles" was available in the New Testament and was to be sharply distinguished from human opinions, even those opinions found in the creeds that were intended to summarize and teach apostolic content. Because he located immersion, for the remission of sins, within "the word of the apostles," he normally understood it to be part of the Christ-given basis for Christian union. How, then, are we to understand the Lunenburg exchange?

In the last lecture I invoked the notion of a catholic ethos. Let me now add a word about context. To catch something of Campbell's vision, in part, requires our understanding enough of his "world-taken-for-granted" to make his vision comprehensible. By the phrase "world-taken-for-granted," I am following Alfred Schuetz and Peter Berger and mean:

> the system of apparently self-evident and self-validating assumptions about the world that each society engenders in the course of its history. This socially determined world view is, at least in part, already given in the language used by the society.[3]

Understanding content requires understanding context. Understanding historical context is, of course, a task that blends into—that really merges with—the comprehension of content because it means recovering a memory of what was philosophically and theologically "understood," implied, or taken for granted, and thus often either unstated or stated in a shorthand way in the discourse of another era.

Several of the most consequential dimensions of Campbell's "world-taken-for-granted" have been summarized by Samuel Pearson in his essay "Faith and Reason in Disciples Theology." He notes that:

> The ideological background of early Disciples thought was the common heritage of all English-speaking Protestant-ism of the eighteenth century, which shaped or limited the treatment of faith and reason by many religious groups...

> Campbell reflects clearly and unambiguously a dependence on the Baconian-Lockean-Newtonian heritage...Campbell...accepted the notion, common in his day, that the Bible is a book of facts which can be used to defend the claims of Christianity.

Pearson goes on to point out that Campbell's philosophical (epistemological) position was "mirrored in the culture of his time" and as yet unchallenged by either "Kantian and post-Kantian" epistemology or more recent forms of biblical criticism.[4]

As a general observation, it is fair to say that late nineteenth and twentieth century philosophy, theology, psychology and, generally, the "world-taken-for-granted" of the United States are no longer so Baconian-Lockean-Newtonian. Moving forward from Campbell's time the context becomes less supportive of his normal assumption that if he could unencumber his listeners' minds (liberate them from prejudices) and teach the facts of the gospel rightly and clearly, they would join him on the platform of his catholic "Plea."

On at least some of the occasions, however, when Campbell's dominant understanding that the "Plea" was right, true, and itself antisectarian was pointedly tested, he would not be absolutist. That which was tested occasionally (on still Baconian-Lockean-Newtonian ground) with Campbell around the issue of immersion baptism was later tested more profoundly and more widely in the movement on different philosophical ground, around issues of sociohistorical biblical criticism and fellowship with the "pious unimmersed."

It is assumed that the vector in the Stone-Campbell Movement that led to the Christian Church (Disciples of Christ) was one that was oriented by its "providential worldview" to be attentive to the activities of Christians and others around them and to discern vocational implications, callings to mission, in those arenas. It is also assumed that this stream of the tradition is one that holds the elements of the "Plea" with the sometimes loosening or de-absolutizing hold of a catholic or holistic ethos.

This leads to three implications: (1) this stream of the movement becomes relatively open to relationship with churches outside its own heritage; (2) the changing definitions and understandings of, and approaches to, mission may be stated in terms of elements of the "Plea," but are significantly driven by those outside relationships and; (3) though rooted in the desire to be "catholic," the ethos of this vector of the movement both contributed to its historical internal divisions and plays into present-day polarizations in the Christian Church (Disciples of Christ).

I shall illustrate this thesis in two basic ways: by a very general overview of the history of Disciples' ecclesiology (especially the understanding of the church beyond-the-local) and by a somewhat more detailed account of Restructure as a focused episode in that history.

Association among congregations in the Stone-Campbell Movement existed in different forms, in both branches of the heritage, prior to the 1832 union. Among the Stoneites there had been pastoral associations after their break with Presbyterianism in 1804. Among the Campbellites, nominally Baptist association participation had prevailed prior to 1830, during the latter part of this period in a distinctive Reformers or Reforming Baptist variety of cooperative support for evangelists such as Walter Scott.

In the 1830s and 1840s the question of cooperative structure beyond the local congregations came to center on a choice between a representative assembly structure, championed by Alexander Campbell after 1830, and a voluntary-subscription-membership-societies plus mass-meeting-convention structure. During this period, Alexander Campbell clearly went beyond "pure" congregationalism in two ways. First, Campbell had come to believe in the legitimacy of a public order of ministry—that of Evangelists. Further, he thought that since the arena of the Evangelist's activity was beyond the local level, the Evangelist's accountability must be extraparochial (beyond the local) as well.[5] Second, Campbell exerted a steady editorial influence through the 1830s and 1840s on behalf of a representative, delegate-composed, national convention for the Disciples.[6]

When the first national convention took place in Cincinnati in 1849, however, it dissolved itself into a mass meeting and created a subscription based voluntary society, the American Christian Missionary Society. The convention also defeated the idea of multicongregational oversight for Evangelists. D. S. Burnet of Cincinnati had already begun to experiment with a number of such societies in Cincinnati and he gave leadership to the organization of the first convention.[7]

The society concept was the basis for national, state, and district level organization among the Disciples in the middle half-century of their history. The trend toward further organizing in this way was hastened by the utter failure of the Louisville Plan of 1869. The Louisville Plan had proposed a delegate structure at district, state, and national levels to be accompanied by an apportioned system of financial support. Neither its representative nor its financial features worked. Thus, the voluntary society concept was the order of the day not only for state and district levels of "cooperative work" but for a wide range of national level organizations.

Until about 1880, the most fruitful fields of Disciples mission were primarily in the United States. The dominant conceptual content of mission was evangelizing in terms of the Disciples "Plea," with a significant degree of proselytizing or what Samuel Hill has called "rectifying."[8] The success of Disciples evangelism in this period seemed to confirm the rightness of this approach.

Clark Gilpin has suggested that the predominant Disciples ecclesiological image (image of church) in this early era was "citizens of the divine kingdom."[9] This image was explicated in Alexander Campbell's thought, employed in Walter Scott's style of evangelism, and echoed by hundreds of other preachers of the "restoration." Within this concept, Jesus Christ appears as the divine monarch and lawgiver.

Although missionary organization had been opposed in some of Campbell's own early writings and these themes echoed by his critics in later years, by and large the context of success, the content of the plea, and the arguments for organizing seemed to many to be congruent. Campbell's own understanding, eventually, was that organizing for mission was done through *covenantal agreements* among churches and that the shape of such organization could be determined by "temporal expediency."[10]

Of course, we are well aware that the legitimacy of such organization came to be one of the bones of sharp contention between members of the movement in the North and those in the South. My focus will remain on the historical stream that moves toward the Christian Church (Disciples of Christ).

In spite of the traumatic reality of growing separation with what were to become the Churches of Christ, organizations beyond the local congregation continued to be born among the Disciples. These included, between 1874 and 1917, two missionary societies, Boards of Church Extension and Education, a Pension Fund, a Council on Christian Unity, and a Benevolent Association. This was the era in which the Disciples grew their organizational "bones and tissue" and they did so on a voluntary-associational framework.

The elaboration of the society concept into so many different organizations with so many different functions had ecclesiological implications. Alexander Campbell had argued for a biblical, "primitive," legitimacy for the Evangelist and for the expediency of organizing for mission. But what was developing in this middle period was a varied array of organization (and their personnel) that expanded well beyond the traditional category of Evangelists.

During the half-century between 1866 and 1917, a number of leaders who had been formed in the Campbellian "Plea," including James H. Garrison, W. T. Moore, and Archibald McLean, developed increasingly interchurch or ecumenical understandings of the movement's traditional commitments to Christian union and missionary evangelization. The participation of Peter Ainslie and a number of other Disciples in the nascent ecumenical movement, the founding of the College of Missions and the development of its life in the consciousness of the world missionary movement as represented by the Edinburgh Conference of 1910, the founding of the Council on Christian Union that same year, all signaled a shift in the interpretation of the Disciples "Plea" toward emphasizing its unity and mission goals and deemphasizing its restoration platform.[11]

The modern ecumenical movement had not been predicated on the Stone-Campbell version of restorationism-union-mission and it was not proceeding on that basis. Its appearance was a new "rock" encountered in the stream of history, then, and different parts of the movement steered differently in response to it.

Disciples who were willing to pursue Christian unity (and mission) on a "non-restorationist" basis could see themselves as recapitulating, on a larger scale, Campbell's occasional setting of a catholic ethos over against an antidenominational "Plea."[12] In the new frame of reference, however, such "transcending" of the "Plea" became the rule and not the exception, and Disciples on this vector have participated in essentially every major ecumenical initiative available to them: the Federal and, later, National Councils of Churches in the United States, the World Council of Churches and its predecessors, bilateral conversations with Baptists, Congregationalists, and the Roman Catholic Church, the Consultation on Church Union, and others.

In addition to this ecumenical conciliar activity, the foreign orientation of the two new missionary societies (Christian Woman's Board of Missions and the Foreign Christian Missionary Society) represented a shifting frame of reference and, eventually, became a source of controversy. Before the 1880s, when Disciples evangelism had a primarily domestic and proselytizing focus,[13] the members of the historic churches were proper objects of missionary activity. But in foreign, predominantly non-Christian fields, members of the historic churches might plausibly be regarded as partners. This was precisely how a segment of Disciples missionaries and missionary executives had come to regard them by the 1920s.[14]

Missionaries associated with the Foreign Department of the (Disciples) United Christian Missionary Society were accused of congregational fellowship with members of nonimmersionist (infant-baptizing) churches. Acrimonious conventions, reaching their apex in the mid-1920s, played out this controversy as some Disciples objected to what they regarded as a compromise relative to the "restored" or New Testament form and meaning of Christian baptism as an integral part of the Disciples historic "Plea."[15]

In 1920 the United Christian Missionary Society was formed from several of the earlier societies (including the American Christian Missionary Society, the Christian Woman's Board of Missions, and the Foreign Christian Missionary Society). The years between 1916 and 1922 were also significant for the development of conventions among Black and Hispanic Disciples.[16]

By the second decade of the twentieth century, then, the organizational shape of Disciples life, and its complexity, far exceeded that of the middle third of the nineteenth century. The locus of mission, missionary philosophy, underlying ecclesiology and predominant christology (understanding or image of Jesus Christ) had also shifted. Foreign mission was the fastest growing field of effort, in rate of growth and prominence in popular imagination if not in absolute numbers. Progressive Protestant Christianity, rather than the "Plea," was the essential message in words and, increasingly, in educational and medical service deeds.[17]

"The Brotherhood" was, as Clark Gilpin reminds us, the primary ecclesiological image during this period.[18] And this image, though normally applied to internal relationships, resounded congruently with the increasingly "world" and interchurch approach to mission. Allen Van Dozier Eikner has shown that the ascendant christological image of this period among Disciples progressives, rooted in part in their increasing contact with a wider Protestant liberalism, was that of the "personal Christ."[19]

It seems clear the shift to this more cooperative, interchurch, and global approach to mission was significantly carried forward by the women of the Disciples, especially through the Christian Woman's Board of Missions. One of the ironies of the "Brotherhood" image is that this familial feeling and understanding of church life was so prominently embodied by the sisters! It also was the case that these sisters rooted their mission activity in a broad, providential worldview. Lexingtonian and historian of the CWBM Ida Withers Harrison had this to say:

> One of the needs of today is a vision that looks beyond the superficial and extraneous and sees the secret springs that are moving women in their united efforts for the betterment of our land, and of all the world.[20]

Note the juxtaposition of language about "secret springs" (providence) and language about "all the world" as the locus of mission.

In the 1930s, '40s, and '50s, cooperative Disciples launched a series of interagency bodies to coordinate the work of the various societies (now termed "agencies") that had emerged in the previous generations. These interagency bodies included Unified Promotion (for the coordination of fundraising), Home and State Missions Planning Council, National Church Program Coordinating Council (for the coordination of program), the Curriculum and Program Council and the Christian Education Assembly (for the coordination of Christian education). In 1950 the most comprehensive of the interagency bodies, the Council of Agencies, was formed and it was from this body that a significant part of the formal impetus to Restructure eventually came.

Meanwhile in the 1940s, the International Convention of Disciples of Christ created a Commission on the Restudy of the Disciples of Christ that drew its membership from across the spectrum of the emerging camps in the remaining movement. A continued commitment to the restoration idea and to the attendant self-understanding as "movement" rather than church or denomination appears in this Commission's reports. There was also a minority report, however, that advocated the softening of the restoration emphasis and the forthright embrace of denominational status by the Disciples of Christ.[21]

About a decade after the Commission on Restudy, the Board of Higher Education and the United Christian Missionary Society (both unambiguously cooperative) convened a Panel of Scholars. This Panel's reports, published in 1963, reversed the dominant note that the Commission on Restudy had sounded. In fact, this Panel's reporting was one of the avenues through which the idea of restoration or Christian primitivism was thoroughly criticized.

Restorationism's traditional Disciples form was depicted in these volumes as untenable in the light of biblical scholarship and in terms of an historical consciousness. Perhaps most tellingly, restorationism was depicted as detrimental to the achievement of Christian unity.[22] The Panel's reports were published at a time when ecumenical enthusiasm (associated especially with the Second Vatican Council and the launching of the Consultation on Church Union) was running high. In some circles this atmosphere added support to the notion that ecumenism (and not restoration) was the path to Christian unity and in other circles it became a source of deep concern.

On the local level, congregations were adopting a "functional church organization" that had been set forth in a book by O. L. Shelton of Butler University and that was promoted by the Home and State Missions Planning Council.[23] This was a scheme that diminished the roles of (the purportedly biblical or primitive) eldership and diaconate and enhanced the roles of the (by now often professionally trained) minister and "functional departments." It could be argued that the widespread congregational adoption of "functional organization" was a structural repudiation of primitivism/restorationism that parallelled primitivism's ideological repudiation that was clear in the reports of the Panel of Scholars.

Excursus on Barton W. Stone in "Progressive" Memory

On one level, the criticism and repudiation of the restoration dimension of the Disciples "Plea" may seem to have been a dramatic reversal of Disciples tradition. And it is a significant theological development of this stream of the movement. But I have tried to show that it rested on gradual, experienced changes in the frame of reference.

It also rested on active reinterpretations and reappropriations of the movement's past. This may be briefly illustrated with reference to the way a founder, Barton Stone, was remembered.

Of course, as with any figure, the historical events of Stone's life were recounted—his birth in Maryland, his education in North Carolina, his entering Presbyterian ministry, his involvement with McGready, his coming to central Kentucky, his presence and leadership at the sacramental revival meeting here, his family life, his involvement with the Springfield Presbytery and its Last Will and Testament, his troubles and final break with the Presbyterians, his pastoral defense against the inroads of the Shakers, his personal involvement in the union with the Disciples, his untiring editorial, evangelistic, educational, and pastoral labor.

In the generation after 1932, however, there was an unprecedented level of interest in Barton W. Stone. Scholars such as Charles Crossfield Ware, Alonzo Willard Fortune, and E. E. Snoddy were eager to show that their theological liberalism and ecumenism had long and legitimate roots in the Stone-Campbell Movement. Therefore, when they looked at Stone, their gaze was drawn to Stone's questions about the Westminster Confession, Stone's trouble with the Trinity, and Stone's unorthodox view of the Atonement. Because

Fortune and Snoddy had to live with their own conservative critics they identified closely with the Stone who had lived with orthodox critics and opponents. The virtues that Ware, Fortune, and
their colleague Elmer Ellsworth Snoddy saw in Father Stone were
(1) Stone's bold opposition to Calvinist orthodoxy; (2) Stone's practical, reconciling union efforts; and (3) Stone's associational approach to church life.

Because 1932 had been the centennial of the union of the
Disciples and the Christians it was natural to look for and find the
theme of Christian unity in the life of Stone. Further, C. C. Ware
was the longtime "state secretary" for the Disciples in North
Carolina. One feature of the Stoneite churches that Ware found and
commented on was that of the Stoneites' continuing multi
congregation, cooperative associations and ministerial
conferences.[24] It is not surprising that Ware would find this
dimension in Stone's story.

But this generation of scholars had to overlook much in the
Stone of history in order to construct the portrait of him as
progressive ecumenist. Recent studies highlighting Stone's
pessimistic outlook and revivalist theology are needed correctives
to this depiction of a generation ago.[25] As is perennially the case,
history is reconstructed for present needs.

I repeat this material on Stone in this context[26] to illustrate that
the reinterpretation of tradition, its reappropriation, the
highlighting of certain themes in light of contemporary issues, is a
continuing process that reveals shifts in convictions and
understandings. The stream of the movement that was becoming
the Christian Church (Disciples of Christ) had been remembering
features of the movement's story other than the "Ancient Order of
Things" for some time before the reports of the Panel of Scholars
were published. The character of the Barton W. Stone that was "discovered" by early twentieth-century progressive Disciples
disclosed as much about the discoverers as about Stone.

Restructure

The Restructure process and the *Design for the Christian Church
(Disciples of Christ)* sought to address several of those basic questions
with which we began these two lectures: What is the essential
character of the movement? What holds it together or has failed
to? What is its relationship to the wider Christian world, or does
such vocabulary make sense? What is its place in human history
under God?

In a formal way the *Design* responds to each of these things in its "preamble." It identifies the Christian Church (Disciples of Christ) as *a* church within the "universal body of Christ." It claims that its particularity is identifiable by its "tradition, name, institutions, and relationships." It claims to be bound in a "covenant of love" that is "God's."

The *Design* also contains several christological images including: the Christ, Son of the living God, and Lord and Savior of the world. The third paragraph of the *Design* closes this way: "The Christian Church (Disciples of Christ) confesses Jesus Christ as Lord and constantly seeks in all its action to be obedient to his authority."[27]

The Christian Church (Disciples of Christ), then, is *a* church among churches seeking to embody more fully the oneness of *the* Church. Its most pointed christological confession, in the *Design*, echoes both primitive Christianity ("Jesus is Lord") and, more immediately, the primitivism of our peculiar tradition.

But what was the process that yielded this statement? And what unfolded in the fellowship of Disciples within that process? I am approaching the third part of my thesis.

During the 1950s representatives of the agencies of the Christian Churches (Disciples of Christ) engaged in extensive discussions about those agencies' structures and interrelationships. By 1960 the concern and discussions had crystallized into a resolution by the International Convention of Christian Churches (Disciples of Christ) that created a Commission on Brotherhood Restructure. That Commission first met in 1962, and by 1968 it had completed its task of planning, publicizing, writing, and facilitating the adoption of a new "design" for the Christian Churches.

"Restructure" was what the total work of the Commission was called, and it was believed by its proponents to be a way for the Convention to become more efficient and unified for its constituent congregations' corporate efforts in such areas as evangelism, mission, education, stewardship, social action, and benevolence.

At the international level (the United States and Canada), the International Convention of the Christian Churches (Disciples of Christ) became the General Assembly of the Christian Church (Disciples of Christ). The annual gathering of the Convention, at which members of the Christian Churches "convened" was to give way to a biennial assembly of delegates representing congregations, which were now defined as "manifestations" of the one Christian Church (Disciples of Christ).

The church was to be viewed as composed of three "manifestations"—the congregations, the regions, and the general. The basic shape for these manifestations was already in existence—the local churches would be "congregations" now (manifestations of the one church), the old state missionary societies would now be the "regions," and the "general manifestation" would be composed of the old agencies and interagency bodies (with some gradual and partial reorganization).

The most significant new structure created by the *Design* was the broadly representative General Assembly that would be empowered to take final action on recommendations originating from the church's other bodies. This General Assembly would be composed of delegates from congregations, delegates from regions, ordained ministers, "agency" heads, and members of the General Board.[28] Of course, even this significant "new" structure had very important precedents in the former general and international conventions.

The *Design* also provided for a General Board, which would function much as the Committee on Recommendations had functioned. In short, except for the delegate representation (rather than mass meeting of "volunteers") composition of the General Assembly, the structure of the Christian Church (Disciples of Christ) resembles nothing so much as that of the old International Convention of the Christian Churches (Disciples of Christ) and its cooperating organizations.[29]

During the Restructure process, opposition to and advocacy for the emerging *Design* centered in four groups: the leaders of Restructure themselves, the Disciples for Mission and Renewal, the Atlanta Declaration Committee, and the Committee for the Preservation of the Brotherhood. As I have continued to reflect on these four groups during the more than fifteen years since I conducted my dissertation research, I have become convinced that they really represented four alternative readings of the Stone-Campbell movement's vocation that can be expressed in different missionary visions with different accompanying christological emphases or images.

The leaders of Restructure (those working in or with the restructuring bodies) were those who stood in the closest continuity with Disciples organizational and institutional life and its, by then, deep and habitual commitment to and involvement with a wider conciliar ecumenism. They, some reluctantly—others more enthusiastically, relegated restorationism to the historical past and carefully qualified their commitment to the freedom emphasis within Disciples tradition with notions of covenantal responsibility.

Their concept of "covenant" was something less formally theological than the covenant theology beneath Alexander Campbell's dispensationalist understanding of history. It was, however, something more theological than Campbell's "expediency" covenant that had been the ground of cooperation beyond the local congregation in the middle third of the nineteenth century.

The primary commitment of this group clearly revolved around the axis of unity and mission in the Disciples "Plea." Among the Restructure leaders, *unity* was a value cherished both in terms of denominational self-understanding and internal function and as an ecumenical Christian commitment. This group vividly embodied the desire to cherish a version of the Disciples "Plea" that could be held loosely, with the grip of a catholic ethos, but still held.

They also were deeply committed to a church-centered *concept of mission* as it had evolved in the educational, benevolent, homeland, and overseas ministries of Disciples organized life.[30] Their primary christological commitment was therefore, at least implicitly, to Christ as Lord of the Church.

The Disciples for Mission and Renewal were a group "of radical activists [who] were beginning to press for a more secular theology and for commitment to the social program of the New Left."[31] They did not oppose Restructure, but rather feared that it would not go far enough to realize their missional and ecumenical goals. They made their case in fliers distributed at the Disciples International Conventions in the midst of the Restructure process and in their own internal mailings and organizational life. They asserted that the church needed renewal rather than restoration and saw social activism as the source of this renewal.[32]

The Disciples for Mission and Renewal were strongly ecumenically committed and saw the Disciples' traditional commitment to liberty (i.e., congregationalism) as an ecumenical stumbling block and missional impediment. It was their understanding of Christian *mission*, in relatively more social and secular than traditionally church-based terms, that most defined this group in terms of their primary commitment and their main distinction from the leaders of Restructure. Their primary and explicit christological commitment was to Christ as the "Lord of the World."[33]

The Atlanta Declaration Committee saw itself as the "loyal opposition" to Restructure. It organized in Atlanta, Georgia, and made its case through mailings, in its own internal life, and in at least one meeting with representatives of the restructuring bodies. The Atlanta group was headed by a former president of the International Convention and supported by one of the "deans" of the Disciples of Christ historical scholarship of the early twentieth century liberal tradition.

This group advocated an "old-line liberal," "spiritualized," version of restorationism (restoring the religion of [not about] Jesus). They continued to see in this kind of restorationism a possible path to Christian unity.

The Atlanta group was particularly committed to the ideal of liberty in the Disciples "Plea." They advocated Christian unity but insisted that it must be with liberty. In fact, their opposition to Restructure rested largely on the grounds of its alleged connection with the plans of the Consultation on Church Union. They believed that the church's mission was best accomplished under the banner of the "free church" tradition. They were concerned about the "orthodoxy" that had come to the forefront of the ecumenical movement since mid-century.[34] The christological tradition of this group was that of Jesus as "personal savior" often interpreted in terms of late-nineteenth and early twentieth-century liberal progressivism. They were the heirs of the promotion of Barton W. Stone as "liberal" Disciples founder.

The Committee for the Preservation of the Brotherhood was the organizational means by which the perspective of those informally called "independents" was expressed on the Restructure process. This group advocated a *restoration* as the method of pursuing Christian unity, conceived of mission in terms of planting churches "after the New Testament pattern," and upheld liberty in the form of a congregationalism that would exhibit freedom from structures beyond the local congregation.[35]

The commitment to the "Plea" as content, as Truth, and to the "restoration movement" as primary context for mission characterizes this group. The unabated commitment to the restoration platform roots the Committee in a christology that gives significant emphasis to Christ the King, as in the Campbellian "system" and in the rhetoric of Walter Scott.

Thus, during the process of Restructure, groups emerged that both articulated alternative missiological emphases or approaches in the Disciples tradition and rooted them, explicitly or implicitly, in a dominant christological image. These alternatives could not all be equally embraced in Restructure. The proponents of Restructure (the leaders of the process and the Disciples for Mission and

Renewal), for all their differences, shared a common advocacy of the ecumenical movement and organization for mission. Similarly, the opponents of Restructure (the Atlanta Declaration group and the "independents"), for all their differences, shared a common continuing commitment to some form of restorationism and a libertarian suspicion of the ecumenical movement.

In the years since Restructure, the Christian Church (Disciples of Christ) has experienced modest structural change. Ideologically (as evidenced in the literature and "official" actions of the Disciples), the Christian Church (Disciples of Christ) has developed as one would have predicted. That is, the emphases of the Restructure proponents have tended to shape the denomination. The views of the Restructure opponents (even the "loyal" ones—the "old-line liberals") have largely fallen silent or been relegated to the status of historically distant or dissident voices. And, of course, Restructure is regarded by commentators on both sides of the experience to have been the near or virtual completion of the division between the Christian Church (Disciples of Christ) and the "undenominational fellowship of Christian Churches and Churches of Christ."

Therefore, in the interpretation of the "Plea": (1) restorationism has largely been seen as a past method rather than a present option; (2) ecumenical involvement is extolled and pursued as the route to Christian unity; (3) the liberty ideal is qualified very often by notions of responsibility or covenantal obligation; and (4) mission is understood to be evangelistic, ecumenical, and social (i.e., more recent versions of the "secular theology"/New Left emphases are included). The "social amelioration" dimension of Campbell's vision has been remembered.

Not surprisingly, the ecumenical and especially the social conception of mission has been a source of controversy and some polarization in the Disciples since Restructure. This is a locus of polarization predicted by the history of the process.

The emergence in the last generation of Christian Mission Awareness and, later, Disciple Renewal to the ideological/theological right of the denomination's leadership signals significant missiological and christological diversity within the Christian Church (Disciples of Christ). More recently the reorganization of the Disciples Division of Homeland Ministries and reconfiguring of its social action emphasis has resulted in the beginnings of another critique-and-advocacy group to the ideological/theological left of the denomination's leadership. This kind of increasingly apparent theological/ideological diversity lives alongside all the potentially church-dividing pluralisms of the human family and deepens the challenge of expressing oneness in the church.

In this situation, the leadership of the Christian Church (Disciples of Christ), especially General Minister and President Richard Hamm, has read these as times for listening—for trying to discern a vocation or catch a vision for the contemporary Disciples of Christ. A "Process of Discernment" is being proposed to the Christian Church (Disciples of Christ) in General Assembly as an alternative to "Sense of the Assembly" resolutions that had often seemed so polarizing in the past. This proposal says, in part:

> Discernment is more than getting the facts straight, though correct facts are essential to any process of discernment. It is also a matter of being attuned to and led by the Spirit of God, which may lead us to different conclusions than those we have already reached…

Later the proposal calls on Disciples to become a "learning church" equipped with a "means by which to clarify our Christian values and to choose meaningful and well-grounded Christian action."[36]

Some are, frankly, cynical about this proposal. They think it is a dodge from taking what they regard as the "obvious" prophetic stand on this-or-that "tough" social, ethical, or moral issue. But this mild language makes me hopeful, because I hear in this voice shaped by attentiveness, echoes of other voices from our past.

I hear the voice of Thomas Campbell discerning "favorable opportunity" in this "happy land." I hear the voice of Alexander Campbell discerning a providential call to ministry in the ordinary circumstances and extraordinary events of his young manhood. I hear elder and younger Campbell thrilled with and virtually certain of the terms of a "catholic" plea, but unwilling to assert it with exclusive absolutism.

I hear the voices of our mission advocates and leaders changing key, sometimes almost startlingly perhaps, as the wider schemes of providence seemed to demand a catholic, flexible response. I hear, too, the poignancy of voices lamenting lost or broken fellowship because the genuine attempt at faithfulness did not lead all brothers and sisters down the same path.

Those voices from our past make me hopeful, for they are familiar voices and their collective, cumulative messages are: that mission is broad and varied and dynamic; and that Christ is Lord of the Church *and* of the World, personal Savior *and* prophetic Judge of history, *and* still more than tongue can confess; and that we *are* bound in God's covenant of love and that *there* we may yet maintain our unity, and even discover more.

NOTES

[1]Editor [Alexander Campbell], "A Restoration of the Ancient Order of Things. No. I.," *Christian Baptist* 2 (1824–5), 128 (reprint ed., 1835).

[2]Ibid., No. III., 139.

[3]Peter L. Berger, *Invitation to Sociology: A Humanistic Perspective* (Garden City, N.Y.: Anchor Books/Doubleday & Company, Inc., 1963), 117.

[4]Samuel C. Pearson, "Faith and Reason in Disciples Theology," in *Classic Themes of Disciples Theology: Rethinking the Tradition Affirmations of the Christian Church (Disciples of Christ)*, edited and with an introduction by Kenneth Lawrence (Ft. Worth: TCU Press, 1986), 117–18.

[5]A[lexander] C[ampbell], "The Nature of the Christian Organization, No. II," *Millennial Harbinger*, n.s., 6 (February 1842), 62–64.

[6]Anthony L. Dunnavant, "Restructure: Four Historical Ideals in the Campbell-Stone Movement and the Development of the Polity of the Christian Church (Disciples of Christ)" (Ph.D. diss., Vanderbilt University, 1984), 111–15.

[7]See Ralph D. Winter, "Protestant Mission Societies and the 'Other Protestant Schism,'" in *American Denominational Organization: A Sociological View*, ed. Ross P. Scherer (Pasadena, Calif; William Carey Library, 1980), 199; and Conrad Wright, "The Growth of Denominational Bureaucracies: A Neglected Aspect of American Church History," *Harvard Theological Review* 77:2 (1984); 183–85. A book-length account of the Anglo-American tradition of the voluntary societies is Charles I. Foster, *An Errand of Mercy: The Evangelical United Front, 1790–1837* (Chapel Hill: University of North Carolina Press, 1960). The roots of the voluntary society tradition among Disciples have been described by David M. Thompson in "The Irish Background to Thomas Campbell's Declaration and Address," *Discipliana* 46: 2 (Summer 1986), 27, 23. D. S. Burnet's career has been detailed in Noel Keith's *The Story of D. S. Burnet: Undeserved Obscurity* (St. Louis: Bethany Press, 1954).

[8]Samuel S. Hill, "Campbell-Stone on the Frontier: The Only Ones Weren't the Only Ones," in *Lectures in Honor of the Alexander Campbell Bicentennial* (Nashville: Disciples of Christ Historical Society, 1988), 71.

[9]W. Clark Gilpin, "The Integrity of the Church: the Communal Theology of the Disciples of Christ," in *Classic Themes of Disciples Theology*, 32–36.

[10]Dunnavant, "Restructure," 269–70.

[11]Lester G. McAllister and William E. Tucker, *Journey in Faith: A History of the Christian Church (Disciples of Christ)* (St. Louis: Bethany Press, 1975), 322. In his "response" to this lecture, Jerry Rushford noted that James Garfield might be a better name to invoke to illustrate the shift in the thinking and the social location of the Disciples. Professor Rushford's point is well taken.

[12]Dunnavant, "Restructure," 71–72.

[13]On the changing concepts of mission among Disciples, see Don Pittman and Paul Williams "Mission and Evangelism: Continuing Debates and Contemporary Interpretations," in *Interpreting Disciples: Practical Theology in the Disciples of Christ*, ed. L. Dale Richesin and Larry D. Bouchard (Ft. Worth, Tex.: Christian University Press, 1987), 217–19.

[14]The same decade that saw the baptism controversy come to a head, 1917–1927, contained a number of significant structural developments. In 1917 the International Convention of Disciples of Christ was formed. It was a bicameral body

composed of a mass meeting Convention and a delegate Committee on Recommendations. In the same year the National Christian Missionary Convention was formed by African American Disciples, with liaison to the International Convention—to which African American Disciples were formally welcome (McAllister and Tucker, *Journey in Faith*, 342–43). For more detail about the motivation for the African American organization, see Brenda M. Cardwell and William K. Fox, Sr., *Journey Toward Wholeness: A History of Black Disciples of Christ in the Mission of the Christian Church*, vol. 1: *From Convention to Convocation: No Longer "Objects of" Mission But "Partners In" the Work (1700–1988)* (n.p.: National Convocation of the Christian Church [Disciples of Christ], 1990), 28–29.

[15]An account of this controversy is Mark G. Toulouse, "Practical Concern and Theological Neglect: The UCMS and the Open Membership Controversy," in *A Case Study of Mainstream Protestantism: The Disciples' Relation to American Culture: 1880–1989*, ed. D. Newell Williams (St. Louis and Grand Rapids: Chalice Press and William B. Eerdmans Publishing Company, 1991), 194–235.

[16]David A. Vargas, "A Historical Background of the National Hispanic and Bilingual Fellowship," trans. Luis E. Ferrer, *Discipliana* 46: 3 (Fall 1986), 38–39.

[17]Commission for the Direction of Surveys, Authorized by the International Convention of Disciples of Christ, *Survey of Service* (St. Louis: Christian Board of Publication, 1928).

[18]Gilpin, "Integrity of the Church," 37–42. With the prominent use of terms such as "Brotherhood" and "Fellowship," the traditional ecclesiological language of the Disciples sounds quite sexist to many ears in the 1990s. Masculine imagery is unavoidable in the historical records and documents of the Disciples. The writer's own voice will strive for more neutral language.

[19] Allen Van Dozier Eikner, "The Nature of the Church among the Disciples of Christ," (Ph.D. diss., Vanderbilt University, 1962).

[20]Ida Withers Harrison, *The Christian Woman's Board of Missions: 1874–1919* (n.p.:n.p., ca. 1920).

[21]Dunnavant, "Restructure," 73, 74. See also Commission on Restudy of the Disciples of Christ, *Report of the Commission* (San Francisco: International Convention of Disciples of Christ, 1948), 11–15, 26–27 and Webb, *In Search of Christian Unity*, 339–60.

[22]The three most devastating articles with respect to the restoration idea were, in my view, Dwight E. Stevenson, "Concepts of the New Testament Church which Contribute to Dicsiples Thought about the Church," in W. B. Blakemore, general editor, *The Renewal of Church: The Panel of Scholars Reports*, 3 vols. (St. Louis: Bethany Press, 1963), vol. 3: *The Revival of the Churches*, ed. W. B. Blakemore, 38–49; Ralph G. Wilburn, "A Critique of the Restoration Principle: Its Place in Contemporary Life and Thought," in vol. 1: *The Reformation of Tradition*, ed. Ronald Osborn, 215–53; and Ronald Osborn, "Crisis and Reformation: A Preface to Volume I," ibid., 23–30.

[23]Orman L. Shelton, *The Church Functioning Effectively* (St. Louis: Bethany Press, 1946).

[24]For an especially striking instance in C. C. Ware, see his *Barton Warren Stone: Pathfinder of Christian Union—A Story of His Life and Times* (St. Louis: Bethany Press, 1932), 341.

[25]Allen, "Stone that the Builders Rejected"; Hughes, "Apocalyptic Origins of the Churches of Christ." See also D. Newell Williams, "Barton W. Stone's Revivalist Theology," in *Cane Ridge in Context*, ed. Anthony L. Dunnavant with a foreword by James M. Seale (Nashville: Disciples of Christ Historical Society, 1992), 73–92.

[26]The excursus on Barton W. Stone is an abbreviated version of my Cane Ridge Day Address for 1995, "Barton W. Stone: Portraits on the Half-Century."

[27]*The Design for the Christian Church (Disciples of Christ)*, preamble.

[28]"A Provisional Design for the Christian Church (Disciples of Christ)," in *1969 Year Book and Directory (July 1, 1968–June 30, 1969) of the Christian Church (Disciples of*

Christ) (Indianapolis: Christian Church [Disciples of Christ], 1969), 19, 20.

[29]See the table in Dunnavant, *Restructure*, 199–201. Even the shift to delegates for the convention had been put in place before the adoption of the "Provisional Design."

[30]Ibid., 212–17.

[31]Ronald Osborn, "Theological Issues in the Restructure of the Christian Church (Disciples of Christ)," *Mid-Stream* 19:3 (July 1980), 278.

[32]Dunnavant, "Restructure," 17–20.

[33]Disciples for Mission and Renewal, Steering Committee Minutes, 24–25 November 1967, 2.

[34]Ibid., 220–28.

[35]Ibid., 228–34.

[36]*Business Docket and Program: General Assembly, Christian Church Disciples of Christ*, Pittsburgh, Oct. 20–24, 1995, 298.

CHAPTER 3

The Subversion
of Reforming Movements

Richard T. Hughes

Biblical faith is a radical faith and makes radical demands. Yet, in generation after generation, Yahweh's people have gone to extraordinary lengths to tame the biblical God and domesticate his expectations. The Bible tells us that we cannot see God and live. Perhaps that is why we flee from his presence so routinely. When God tells us that he is the Alpha and Omega who transcends our poor ability even to imagine his greatness, we insist on making him over in our own image. When God tells us that he alone can save, we want to save ourselves. When God tells us to serve the poor and the dispossessed, we devote ourselves instead to worship forms and ecclesiastical structures. We substitute dogma for righteousness, orthodoxy for holiness, piety for social transformation, and a whole variety of idols for God himself. Biblical faith *is* a radical faith, but Christians often go to almost any lengths to turn that faith into something conservative, tame, and manageable.

Even when reformers help us to see the true nature of God or point us to the radical demands of the gospel, the historic tendency has always been for their followers to domesticate and compromise that vision within a few short years. I want to explore this tendency by focusing our attention on three Reformation movements of the sixteenth century: Lutheran, Reformed, and Anabaptist. Then, with that context clearly in mind, I want to ask about our own heritage in Churches of Christ. Did we compromise and domesticate the founding vision of our movement? And if so, how and why? Then, I want to ask, if we care at all about the legacy of those founding years, how might we reclaim the most valuable dimensions of that legacy and appropriate those dimensions in our world today?

The Reformed Tradition

The Yale philosopher Nicholas Wolterstorff helps us see the point I wish to make when he reflects in one of his books on the "radical origins" of his own religious heritage. Wolterstorff has lived his entire life in the context of the Reformed tradition of John Calvin. In its earliest years, this tradition sought to implement the radical hope that, somehow, the world might bow the knee to Almighty God and acknowledge Him as ruler and lord. By the grace of God, Christians might then help transform this world into a kingdom of righteousness and justice and peace.

And yet, Wolterstorff recalls that when he grew up in the Reformed tradition he "saw very little of that world formative impulse so prominent in its origins." Instead, his tradition was now content simply to maintain a theological heritage and to nurture a particular style of piety. "The piety," Wolterstorff recalls, "came through most clearly in the prayers," prayers like, "We thank you, Lord, for the many blessings you have granted us, and we ask you to remember those less fortunate than we are." Those prayers, Wolterstorff now recalls, communicated the thought "that it was God's business to take care of the oppressed and deprived of the world; our role was simply to pray that he not neglect to do so." Wolterstorff notes that when he was younger, if someone had told him that Calvinism in its early years actually stood for a radical transformation of the social and political order, he would have found that description "comically perverse."

Since then, Wolterstorff writes, he has discovered the "radical origins" of his tradition. "Learning of those origins has given me a deepened appreciation of my own identity. [But] it has also produced in me a profound discontent over my tradition's loss of its radicalism. Why has it become so quiescently—sometimes even oppressively—conservative?"[1]

The truth is, the pattern Wolterstorff describes here repeats itself in virtually all reforming traditions. The first generation typically promotes a radical vision, rooted squarely in some extraordinary insight into the character of God or grounded in new and fresh understandings of the biblical text. The profundity and depth of that original vision attracts followers who, for various reasons, share that vision and work for its realization. Most often, however, later generations find themselves unable to keep that radical vision alive. As a result, they tame the original vision into a domesticated and manageable ideology, almost entirely shorn of its original power and vibrancy. While the collapse of the original vision may not occur for many years, it sometimes occurs as early as the second or third generation after the original founding.

The Lutheran Tradition

Luther's reform is a notable case in point. As we know, Luther struggled for years with his own sense of guilt. For a host of reasons, the young man Luther could not imagine God in any terms other than judgment and wrath and condemnation. There was no grace, no mercy, no forgiveness. His sense of God's judgment placed on him an enormous burden to achieve perfection and merit God's salvation. And yet, Luther knew his heart and the depth of his own sin. There was no way he could merit God's favor, and no one knew that better than Luther himself. Luther was therefore a terribly troubled man.

But then, while preparing his lectures for a course on the book of Romans, Luther discovered the New Testament understanding of "gospel—" that profoundly biblical doctrine of justification by grace through faith. Slowly it dawned on Luther that he did not have to achieve perfection in order to claim the grace of God. Instead, God extended his grace to Luther simply because God was love, and God had done this in spite of the fact that Luther could never merit this magnificent gift.

This understanding of justification by grace through faith was for Luther no mere "doctrine" that one must believe in order to merit one's salvation. That, of course, would be nothing more than another form of works righteousness. Instead, this doctrine served as a window that opened onto the liberating grace of Almighty God. Put another way, here was a *particular* biblical vision, but one that broke through its own particularity to allow the young man Luther to feel and experience and know the love and the grace of God. Put yet another way, the doctrine was not the critical issue here, but rather the God to whom the doctrine pointed. For this reason, justification by grace through faith became for Luther a dynamic, life-giving, liberating, and soul-transforming vision.

And yet, by the end of the sixteenth century, some of Luther's followers had transformed the notion of justification by grace through faith into nothing more than a doctrine to which one had to give intellectual assent in order to maintain one's status as an orthodox Lutheran. These people came to be known as Lutheran Scholastics. As far as the doctrine of justification by grace through faith was concerned, the issue for them was not so much the God to whom the doctrine pointed, but rather the doctrine itself. They were far less concerned for transformation of life than for maintenance of Lutheran orthodoxy. As one of my professors at the University of Iowa said many years ago, the Scholastic theologians embroidered onto a fine piece of cloth the words, "Justification by Grace Through Faith," then framed the cloth and hung it on the church-house wall and asked the congregation, "Do you believe it? Because if you don't you're not a good Lutheran."

In many ways the Scholastics had moved 180 degrees away from Luther's original vision, even though they used the very same language Luther had used some years before. But why? Why did this radical transformation occur? One reason seems obvious. Luther's reforming movement by the end of the sixteenth century had become an institution in its own right. There can be no question that some felt the need to transform Luther's original vision into an orthodox, dogmatic formulation that could clearly mark the boundary separating Lutherans both from Catholics and from other Protestants.

But I suspect there is more to the story than this. Luther's understanding of justification by grace through faith carried with it the requirement that one recognize one's self as sinful, alienated, broken, and estranged both from God and from other human beings. This is precisely why we are justified by grace and not by works. But how difficult it is to confess and embrace our own sinful nature! How much easier it is to invent strategies by which we can justify ourselves! The motivation must have been powerful, then, to transform the radical notion of justification by grace through faith into a simplistic dogma that one must believe in order to achieve one's own salvation. While it might be difficult to confess one's sins, it was far easier to say, "I believe in the proposition that I am justified by grace through faith." That, the Scholastics imagined, was a quick and easy ticket through the pearly gates.

Without question, the Scholastics preserved the form and even the words of the founding vision, but their understanding of justification by grace through faith had little or nothing to do with Luther's original insight. In effect, they transformed God himself into a tame, manageable, and thoroughly domesticated deity who now had to respond in positive ways to their own affirmations of orthodoxy. Put another way, God was now little more than a puppet on a string. And most striking of all, these changes transpired within seventy-five years of the founding generation.

The Anabaptist Tradition

We find the very same dynamics at work in another tradition of the Reformation period: the sixteenth-century Anabaptists. The vision that inspired this movement was so radical that the people who embraced it were known as the "radicals of the Reformation." What did they seek? What was their vision? What was their dream?

The story began in Zürich, Switzerland, in 1523. Huldreich Zwingli, the pastor of the newly reformed Protestant church of that city, urged his congregation to ignore the traditions of the church and the medieval theologians, but to focus instead on the biblical text. That, of course, was a risky challenge for Zwingli to make, since anyone who takes the Bible seriously risks being radicalized by the biblical message.

Not surprisingly, some in Zwingli's congregation took his challenge to heart. As they read the New Testament, and especially the gospels, these people discovered the enormous gap between the teachings of Jesus and the world of sixteenth-century Christendom. On the one hand, Jesus made radical demands. He told his followers, or would-be followers, to find power not in their swords but in suffering and the cross, to sell what they had and give to the poor, to leave mother and father and brothers and sisters and follow him exclusively, to find themselves by losing themselves, and to abandon themselves for the sake of the poor and the dispossessed. Yet, the popular church in sixteenth-century Europe knew little or nothing of this kind of witness.

The problem—according to these Anabaptists—was simply the state church. This arrangement meant that every child born into a European family was automatically enrolled in the state church by virtue of his or her baptism that took place just a few days after the child's birth. Some of these children, of course, grew up to be murderers or thieves or adulterers or liars, or just people without any meaningful commitment to the Christian faith. And yet, they were still in the church.

But those who would soon be known as Anabaptists wanted a church composed *only* of people committed to living out the radical teachings of Jesus. In point of fact, these people sought nothing more nor less than a restoration of primitive Christianity. But for them, the touchstone for understanding the ancient Christian faith was not so much the book of *Acts* as the teachings of Jesus in the Gospels. They hoped to create a community that would triumph not by the sword but by the cross and by the principle of nonresistance; a community that would shun wealth and status; and a community whose members would care for each other in very concrete ways, but especially for the poor and the dispossessed.

In order to create this kind of radical Christian community, these people proposed to Zwingli that the church in Zürich abandon the practice of infant baptism and adopt instead the baptism of adults, but only those adults committed to a radical Christian witness. This vision meant that alongside the state church there would exist a separate church, composed only of committed believers.

It is difficult for us to comprehend today what a revolutionary proposal this was. It was revolutionary because it meant a break with the traditional pattern of the state church, a pattern that had dominated all of Europe for almost 1,200 years. For all that time, the state church had been the glue that bound Christian society into one united Christendom. No one could imagine giving up this commitment. And the possibility that people might have the freedom to choose between a state church and a separate church of convicted believers was a thought that boggled the minds of most who gave it any consideration.

And so, when Zwingli received the proposal that the Zürich church adopt the practice of baptism of adults, he wisely referred it to the Zürich town council for a decision. After considerable debate, the council finally ruled: there would be no adult baptisms, and anyone who either baptized another person as an adult, or submitted to baptism as an adult, would be executed.

In spite of that ruling, there were people committed to living their lives as Jesus taught them to live and who refused to be intimidated. And so, on January 21, 1525, several of those met together and prayed to God for courage to do what should be done. Then, as the *Hutterite Chronicle* tells us, "George Cajacob arose and asked Conrad [Grebel] to baptize him…After that was done, the others similarly desired George to baptize them, which he also did upon their request." And then, the *Chronicle* tersely notes, "Therewith began the separation from the world and its evil works."[2]

Therewith also began the executions of Anabaptists all over Europe. How many died in all, we shall never know. But they died by the thousands—executed by the sword, burned at the stake, drowned, and murdered in a variety of hideous ways.

The story of Dirk Willems, a Dutch Anabaptist, typifies the way the founding generation sought to restore the practical implications of the gospel of Jesus Christ. Like so many other Anabaptists, Willems spent considerable time on the run, but the authorities finally caught him and put him in prison, there to await his execution. But on a bitterly cold winter's day, Willems managed to escape by dropping from a window on a rope of knotted rags. Once on the ground, he scampered across the sheet of ice that covered the prison moat. Suddenly he heard the prison guard behind him. Willems ran as fast as he could run. But then, he heard a piercing scream. When he looked, he saw the guard who had fallen through the ice and was now desperately calling for help. What would you have done? Kept running? Willems turned around, walked carefully back across the icy moat, and rescued the guard from certain death. Once freed from the grip of the icy waters, the guard seized Willems, bound him, and led him back to prison. A few days later, Dirk Willems burned at the stake.[3]

One hundred and fifty years after Willems' death, much had changed among these Anabaptists. One noted historian writes that by then "the creative and intellectual character of Anabaptism had already vanished."[4] In that climate, a young zealot named Jacob Ammann radically redefined the meaning of Anabaptism. Anabaptists for years had excommunicated those who failed to take seriously the radical standards of the Christian faith, but Ammann argued that all excommunicated persons should be completely shunned. Ammann also argued that anyone guilty of speaking a falsehood should be forthwith cut off from the church. He further claimed that Christians who shared Anabaptist convictions and helped them in time of persecution could not be saved so long as they remained outside the Anabaptist fold. Finally, "Ammann condemned the trimming of the beard and the wearing of gay clothing, and 'anyone desiring to do so,' he said, 'shall be justly punished.'"[5] On these points, Ammann began to divide the Anabaptist congregations. At a meeting in Niklaus Moser's barn, Ammann excommunicated a sizable group of ministers who refused to conform to his demands, then walked out, refusing to shake the hands of those whom he had expelled.[6] With this action began the historic tradition we know today as the Amish.

Today, the Amish in the United States seldom distinguish themselves by the drive to restore to their lives the radical teachings of Jesus. Instead, they have committed themselves to the preservation of traditional folkways. They do embrace simplicity and nonresistance. But they have so completely segregated themselves from the larger world that these fundamental gospel virtues have lost their power to speak in meaningful ways to the world in which they live. The world knows them best for their quilts, for their resistance to modernization, for their habits of dress, and especially perhaps for their rejection of the automobile in favor of the old-fashioned horse and buggy. The Amish are good and simple people, and admirable in many ways, but their forebears' commitment to the kind of radical Christian witness that reaches beyond the household of faith to serve a world in need has, for the most part, disappeared.

Commonalities

For all their differences, John Calvin, Martin Luther, and that first generation of Anabaptists shared in common one fundamental commitment. Each was driven by a powerful vision of God. In a period when a church grown too fat and powerful had presumptuously pushed God from His throne, Luther, Calvin, and the Anabaptists were each committed in some important way to allow God to be God once again. For this reason, each extracted from the biblical text a theology that opened a window on the power, or the grace, or the goodness, or the love of God. This was precisely what made each of these movements radical and why each was so effective in its own time. None of these movements committed itself to maintain a mere institution, an ideology, or an orthodoxy of some kind. Instead, each was committed to God and sought to translate God's power, or rule, or goodness, or grace into the common culture of sixteenth-century Europe.

If we were to ask what specific forms those visions took, it is clear that Calvin affirmed God's sovereign rule over all the earth, Luther affirmed the fact that God alone can save, while the Anabaptists embraced a commitment to radical discipleship and in that way, allowed the grace of God to manifest itself in their daily lives.

In the founding generations of those traditions, forms and structures and doctrines seldom became ends in themselves, but served instead to point beyond themselves to the source who gives forms and structures and doctrines their meaning. That source, of course, is God. Put another way, while each of these traditions constituted a particular movement with a particular theology and a particular slant on the Christian gospel, each was able to break through its own particularity to allow believers to see and hear and feel the only legitimate focus of Christian faith, namely, God Himself.

And yet, in all three instances, followers in later years subverted their own traditions precisely because they substituted lesser things for the vision of God that had driven the founding generations. The Reformed tradition substituted piety and academic theology. The Lutheran tradition substituted scholastic formulations and orthodoxies. And the Amish embraced outward apparel, untrimmed beards, and a legal approach to the Christian faith that effectively displaced the original commitment to radical discipleship.

These "lesser things" shared one thing in common. Each represented an effort to tame the living God and put God in a box. And yet, above all other considerations, God is a free and living God who breaks out of our boxes, who transcends our efforts to capture His essence, who cannot be contained by our thoughts and theological formulations, no matter how biblical we may think them to be. How can one possibly encompass God in a particular form of piety? In a scholastic form of orthodoxy? In legal regulations or rules about beards and apparel? How can one tame or manage or domesticate the free and living God?

The tragedy of the various forms and structures embraced by later Calvinists, Lutherans, and Anabaptists lay in the fact that they possessed little or no ability to break through their own particularity. Instead, they often became ends in themselves. Too often, they functioned as roadblocks that obscured the glory of God from the longing eyes of believers, not as windows that allowed God's love and grace to flood the hearts and souls of His people.

Churches of Christ

With this background, then, what might we say about Churches of Christ?

First, we must ask, what was the driving genius of our tradition in its early years? Disciples of Christ argue that the heart and soul of this tradition was its ecumenical thrust, its drive toward Christian unity. On the other hand, Churches of Christ have claimed that the fundamental thrust of this movement has been its passion to restore the ancient Christian faith.

The Meaning of Our Movement:
The Freedom to Search for Truth

There is merit in both those claims, but I want to argue that neither of these themes stands at the heart and soul of the movement to which Alexander Campbell, Barton W. Stone, Elias Smith, and James O'Kelley gave birth in the early years of the nineteenth century. Instead, ours was essentially a freedom movement, designed to liberate the minds of men and women from static and oppressive systems, from the boxes into which various theological tyrants had sought to place not only God but their followers as well, and from the hard and brittle molds into which little minds had attempted to compress the liberating gospel of Jesus Christ. Put another way, the founders of our movement were committed to a relentless search for truth, and that commitment in many ways defined the meaning of the tradition.

In my judgment, one of the finest books on the history of Churches of Christ published in the past fifty years is a book that deals not with the history of Churches of Christ *per se*, but with the history of popular religion in the United States in the early nineteenth century, a story that includes the Churches of Christ along with a variety of other popular religious traditions. Authored by Nathan O. Hatch and appearing in 1989, that book is entitled, *The Democratization of American Christianity*. Likewise, one of the finest articles dealing with the history of our tradition is also by Hatch. Published in *The Journal of American History* in 1980, that article bears the title, "The Christian Movement and the Demand for a Theology of the People." An outsider to Churches of Christ, and previously unfamiliar with the way we view the world, Hatch was simply stunned by the ringing affirmations of freedom that characterized the founding generation. He was incredulous, for example, that some of Barton Stone's early colleagues could write, "We are not personally acquainted with the writings of John Calvin, nor are we certain how nearly we agree with his views of divine truth; neither do we care." After rehearsing this and other affirmations of Christian freedom offered by our forebears,[7] Hatch finally exclaimed,

This was no mere revolt against Calvinism but [a revolt] against theology itself. What was going on that gave [Barton W.] Stone the audacity not only to reject the doctrine of the Trinity...but also to maintain, "I have not spent, perhaps, an hour in ten years in thinking about the Trinity"? What made it credible for [Elias] Smith, after seriously debating whether he would be a Calvinist or a Universalist, to remove the dilemma altogether by dropping them both? "I was now without a system," he confessed with obvious relief, "and felt ready to search the scriptures."...Whatever else the Christians demanded,...they called for a new dispensation of gospel liberty, radically discontinuous with the past.[8]

Hatch is right. Even a cursory review of the early literature produced by the founders of our movement reflects their preoccupation with Christian freedom and the right of every Christian to search for truth. Alexander Campbell, for example, made this very characteristic affirmation in 1827:

I have been so long disciplined in the school of free inquiry, that, if I know my own mind, there is not a man upon the earth whose authority can influence me, any farther than he comes with the authority of evidence, reason, and truth....I have endeavored to read the scriptures as though no one had read them before me; and I am as much on my guard against reading them today, through the medium of my own views yesterday, or a week ago, as I am against being influenced by any foreign name, authority, or system, whatever.[9]

Many in Churches of Christ today may not discern how radical this kind of rhetoric really is. This is why we must listen to those like Nathan Hatch who found this kind of rhetoric almost shocking. When Hatch read this comment from Campbell, he exclaimed, "Protestants had always argued for *sola scriptura*, but this kind of radical individualism set the Bible against the entire history of biblical interpretation."[10]

And yet, one finds this emphasis not just in Alexander Campbell, but also in Barton Stone. In *The Last Will and Testament of the Springfield Presbytery*, by virtue of which Stone and five of his colleagues proclaimed their freedom in Jesus Christ, one finds these stunning statements.

> We *will*, that our power of making laws for the government
> of the church, and executing them by delegated authority,
> forever cease; that the people may have free recourse to
> the Bible, and adopt *the law of the Spirit of life in Christ Jesus.*

Or again,

> We *will*, that the Synod of Kentucky examine every mem-
> ber, who may be *suspected* of having departed from the
> Confession of Faith, and suspend every such suspected
> heretic immediately; in order that the oppressed may go
> free, and taste the sweets of gospel liberty.[11]

That document was published on June 28, 1804. Twenty-two
years later, Stone was still consumed with a passion for Christian
freedom. He wrote, for example, in 1826,

> We must be fully persuaded, that all uninspired men are
> fallible, and therefore liable to err...Luther, in a coarse
> manner, said *that every man was born with a Pope in his belly.*
> By which I suppose he meant, that every man deemed him-
> self infallible....If the present generation remain under the
> influence of [this]...principle, the consequences must be,
> that the spirit of free enquiry will die—our liberty lie pros-
> trated at the feet of ecclesiastical demagogues...[12]

Likewise, some of Stone's followers contended in 1826 for "certain inalienable rights." And what were those rights? The rights of
"free investigation, [and] sober and diligent inquiry after truth."[13]

These are impressive statements, but none was more impressive than the warning offered by John Rogers, the preacher for the
Church of Christ in Carlisle, Kentucky, during the earliest years of
the nineteenth century. "The *fatal error* of all reformers," Rogers
wrote,

> has been that they have too hastily concluded that they
> knew the whole truth, and have settled back upon the same
> principles of proscription, intolerance and persecution,
> against which they so strongly remonstrated...Having,
> then, full in our view, this fatal rock, on which so many
> reformers have split, may we studiously avoid it. We have
> no reason to conclude, we know all the truth...We have
> nothing to lose in this inquiry after truth. We have no sys-
> tem to bind us to human opinions.[14]

When one grasps the passion with which the founding generation of Churches of Christ defended what they called the "inalienable right" to search for truth, so much else comes into focus. For example, in the early years of his reform, Alexander Campbell ruthlessly attacked the clergy of the various denominations. But he did so, not because he thought they were wrong on various fine points of theology. Instead, he attacked the clergy because their narrow and provincial dogmatism so often prevented their followers from exercising their "inalienable right" to search for truth. As Campbell noted in 1823, "No class or order of men that ever appeared on earth have obtained so much influence, or acquired so complete an ascendency over the human mind, as the clergy."[15]

One might make the very same point about the protest against creeds that characterized Churches of Christ in their early years. The problem with creeds lay in the fact that they codified truth, and in that way, shut off any further need to search for further light on a given topic. Put another way, creeds put God in a box. Precisely for this reason, the founding generation never intended that rejection of creeds should become a major plank in the unwritten creed of later generations of Churches of Christ. That this has happened time and again is the supreme irony of our movement and only demonstrates how far we have come from the ideals of the founding generation. The truth is, the founders' rejection of creeds was nothing more than an affirmation of the right to search for truth.

On Letting God Be God

But how does all of this connect with Luther, Calvin, and the Anabaptists? Did the search for truth that characterized the founders of our tradition have anything in common with the fundamental goals of those three reforming movements? The answer to that question is a resounding "yes." Our founders shared with Luther, Calvin, and the Anabaptists an intense desire for all men and women simply to let God be God. Calvin expressed this commitment in his affirmation of God's sovereignty over all the earth. Luther expressed this commitment in his affirmation that human beings are justified only by God's grace. And the Anabaptists expressed this commitment in their determination to live out God's sovereign grace in their common lives.

But what of Churches of Christ? Our founders expressed their determination to let God be God in their insistence that no human being can capture the truth, possess the truth, codify the truth, preserve the truth, dispense the truth, or guard the truth. Instead, each of us must search for truth, and that search is a search that is never completely finished. This was a powerful way of confessing that human beings are finite and frail and limited not only in their moral attainments but even in their understanding. This was also a powerful way of confessing that God alone is truth and stands in righteous judgment on all human pretensions to capture the truth, as if the truth could be possessed like a car or a house or a pair of trousers. After all, God is the God who continually shatters the boxes in which we seek to contain Him. This is why the founders of our tradition always insisted that the search for truth is an inalienable right of every human being and one that is never brought to completion.

Once we understand that the commitment to search for truth was first and foremost a commitment to the sovereignty of Almighty God, we can then discern why that commitment defined virtually every other theme in our movement. The restoration vision is a case in point. In the hands of the founders of our movement, the restoration vision challenged and rebuked those who smugly assumed that their creeds and systems had captured the essence of the Christian faith. In the early years of our movement, the restoration vision was a stick of intellectual dynamite that exploded those assumptions and said to those who made such arrogant claims, "You are a human being, and you cannot possibly encompass the mind of Almighty God." The restoration vision therefore sent everyone back to the biblical text time and time again.

Yet, when divorced from the right to search for truth, the restoration vision could quickly become a mockery and a sham. Some in those early years, for example, thought the restoration vision a requirement that *others* return to the biblical text time and again, but not themselves, since they had long since found the truth, embraced the truth as a possession, and restored the ancient church in all its purity and perfection. Yet, if we judge by the genius of the restoration vision as framed by the founders of our movement, we must conclude that the restoration vision is legitimate only so long as we conceive of the restoration task as process and search. If we imagine we have fully restored the ancient church, or if we think there is no longer any reason to search for truth, we have at that point turned our backs on the very restoration heritage we claim to embrace.

In much the same way, the passion to search for truth also shaped the other major commitment of our movement, namely, the commitment to help achieve the tangible union of all Christian people. As envisioned by the founders of our movement, this ecumenical thrust never depended on the ability of human beings to arrive at the truth or to agree on a set of theological propositions. Instead, it depended, first, on the fact that God is God and that by His grace alone, Christian people are bound to one another; and, second, on the ability of human beings to recognize that they are not God and must therefore never behave as though they are.

Thomas Campbell spelled out the first of these principles in the cornerstone of the Christian movement, the *Declaration and Address*, published in 1809. There Thomas wrote:

> All that are enabled *through grace* [italics mine] to make…a profession [of faith in Jesus Christ], and to manifest the reality of it in their tempers and conduct, should consider each other as the precious saints of God, should love each other as brethren, children of the same family and Father, temples of the same Spirit, members of the same body, subjects of the same grace, objects of the same Divine love, bought with the same price, and joint-heirs of the same inheritance. Whom God hath thus joined together no man should dare to put asunder.[16]

The critical terms in this statement are these: "subjects of the same grace," "objects of the same Divine love," "bought with the same price," and "joint-heirs of the same inheritance." Why are Christians one? Because God is God, and because He has extended to each of us the very same grace and bought us all with the very same price.

But the ecumenical thrust of our movement was also rooted in the other side of this coin, namely, the conviction that while God is God, all human beings are sinful and finite and frail. It is therefore inevitable that all human beings, including those who belong to Churches of Christ, will make mistakes, misunderstand the word of God, and misappropriate the truth. If that is so, our founders argued, then we must bear with one another's limitations in tolerance and mutual understanding. There can be no more powerful motivation for the unity of all Christian people than this.

Listen, for example, to Barton W. Stone. "I have too much evidence of my liability to err," Stone confessed, "to make my present opinions a test by which to judge the hearts of my fellow Christians." Or again, he wrote, "Be careful not to wound the feelings of the least Christian of any name. View all the children of God as your brethren, whatever name they may bear. What, if they have received wrong opinions of truth? This is no reason why you should despise or reject them. Consider the best method of correcting those errors." It was for this reason that Stone could affirm as late as 1841, "It is common with us that Baptists, Methodists and Presbyterians commune with us, and we with them."[17] Stone made this statement as an aged man, forty years after he broke with the Synod of Kentucky and helped dissolve the Springfield Presbytery in order to take his stand as a simple New Testament Christian. But the stand he took as a simple New Testament Christian never prevented him from embracing a variety of Christian people who simply failed to see the truth from Stone's particular angle of vision. Here we find the meaning of that classic affirmation: "Christians only, but not the only Christians."

Conclusions

What, then, have I tried to say about the genius of the movement that finally resulted in the body of believers we know today as the Churches of Christ? It is obvious that the founders of our movement announced two immediate goals: the restoration of the ancient church and the unity of all Christian people. But I have tried to suggest that the genius of our tradition in its early years lay not in these particular goals, but rather in its frank recognition that God alone is God and that all human beings are fallible. In this recognition, the "reformation of the nineteenth century," as Alexander Campbell liked to call it, stood shoulder to shoulder in very important ways with the great reformation movements of the sixteenth century—those of Luther, Calvin, and the Anabaptists.

The recognition that God alone is God and that all human beings are fallible served our movement in many ways. It served the goal of Christian union since it allowed the founders to join hands with a host of Christian people in a common search for truth. And it served the goal of restoration since it implicitly argued that every Christian must return to the biblical text time and time again, constantly rethinking his or her beliefs and opinions in the light of God's holy word. This is precisely what Campbell meant when he wrote in 1827 that he had "endeavored to read the scriptures as though no one had read them before" him, and that he kept up his "guard against reading them to-day, through the medium of…[his] own views yesterday, or a week ago." And finally, the recognition that God is God and all human beings are fallible graced Churches of Christ with a profound humility and openness that allowed them to break through their own particularity, even while attempting to recover some very concrete particulars of the ancient Christian faith.

But like the Lutherans, the Calvinists, and the Anabaptists of later years, members of Churches of Christ found it difficult to keep their original vision alive. Within a few short years, some had essentially abandoned the search for truth. Instead, they now began to claim they had fully recovered the truth and restored the ancient church. They elevated their rejection of creeds to the status of a creedal statement, and attacked those who failed to see the truth from their particular angle of vision. For all practical purposes, these people had turned their backs on the genius of their own tradition: the conviction that God is God and all human beings are fallible.

Next, I want to explore how and why this transition occurred. But more than that, I want to ask how it might be possible for us to recover this profoundly valuable legacy that allowed Churches of Christ in their early years to affirm the judgment of God, but also his grace; to affirm the restoration of ancient Christianity, but also the unity of all Christians; and to face both the world and God with openness, humility, and a commitment to maintain a constant search for truth.

NOTES

[1]Nicholas Wolterstorff, *Until Justice and Peace Embrace* (Grand Rapids: Eerdmans, 1983), ix.

[2]*Die Alteste Chronik der Hutterischen Bruder*, 45–47, in Hans J. Hillerbrand, ed., *The Reformation: A Narrative History* (New York: Harper and Row, 1964), 230–231.

[3]John S. Oyer and Robert S. Kreider, eds., *Mirror of the Martyrs* (Intercourse, Pa.: Good Books, 1990), 36–37.

[4]John A. Hostetler, *Amish Society*, rev. ed. (Baltimore: Johns Hopkins University Press, 1963), 27.

[5]Ibid., 34.

[6]Ibid., 31.

[7]Nathan O. Hatch, *The Democratization of American Christianity* (New Haven: Yale University Press, 1989), 68–78; and Hatch, "The Christian Movement and the Demand for a Theology of the People," *Journal of American History*, 67 (December 1980), 545–57.

[8]Hatch, "The Christian Movement," 557.

[9]Alexander Campbell, "Reply [to Robert Baylor Semple]," *Christian Baptist*, 3 (April 3, 1826), 229.

[10]Hatch, "The Christian Movement," 559–60.

[11]Barton W. Stone, et al., "The Last Will and Testament of the Springfield Presbytery," in Charles A. Young, ed., *Historical Documents Advocating Christian Union* (Chicago: The Christian Century, 1904), 20–22.

[12]Stone, n.t., *Christian Messenger* 1 (November 25, 1826), 2.

[13]J. and J. Gregg, "An Apology for Withdrawing from the Methodist Episcopal Church," *Christian Messenger* 1 (December 25, 1826), 39–40.

[14]John Rogers, "The Church of Christ at Concord, to the Elders and Brethren Assembled in Conference at Caneridge, Sendeth Christian Salutation," *Christian Messenger* 4 (October 1830), 258.

[15]Campbell, "The Christian Religion: The Clergy No. I," *Christian Baptist* 1 (October 6, 1823), 49.

[16]Thomas Campbell, "Declaration and Address," in Young, *Historical Documents*, 112.

[17]Stone, "Dr. Worcester on the Atonement," *Christian Messenger* 4 (December 1829), 3; "Letter to J.C.," *Christian Messenger* 4 (September 1830), 226; and "Reply to the Above," *Christian Messenger* 11 (June 1841), 340.

CHAPTER 4

The Taming of the Restoration Tradition

Richard T. Hughes

Previously, I tried to make the case that the driving genius of Churches of Christ in our early years was our commitment to the conviction that "God is God and all human beings are fallible." This commitment expressed itself in the unrelenting search for truth that characterized the founding generation.

Yet, within a few short years, a large number of people in our tradition had exchanged that search for a preoccupation with lesser things. Some claimed they no longer needed to search for truth since they now possessed the truth in its fullness. Others argued there was no longer a need to restore the ancient church since the ancient church had been completely restored and now existed in the form of congregations of Churches of Christ that dotted the landscape of the nineteenth-century American frontier. What was needed, these people claimed, was a valiant effort to defend the gains of the past.

The striking thing about Churches of Christ was how quickly this transition transpired. In the case of Lutherans, Calvinists, and Anabaptists, this kind of transition took place by the third, fourth, or fifth generation. In the case of Churches of Christ we find unmistakable signs of this transition in the movement's earliest years.

At present, I want to ask two questions: (1) What evidence do we have that this transition did, in fact, occur? And (2) what can we do now to reverse that transition and reclaim the genius of our own religious heritage?

It is a simple matter to document that a major transition did occur during our movement's earliest years. If we ask where the responsibility for that transition lies, we must conclude that it lies, at least in part, at the feet of Alexander Campbell himself. It is true that Campbell promoted an unrelenting search for truth when he announced, for example, that he tried to read the scriptures "as though no one had read them before" and that he tried every day to hear the biblical message afresh.

At the same time, by making extravagant claims regarding the nature of his own movement, Campbell helped to subvert the genius of his own vision. For example, he argued in 1830 that "no seven years of the last ten centuries" had done more to hasten the millennial age than had "the last seven" years when he had produced his paper, the *Christian Baptist*. Then, in 1835, Campbell announced that his movement had actually recovered biblical truth and restored the ancient church. "Various efforts have been made," he announced, "and considerable progress attended them, but since the Grand Apostasy was completed, till the present generation, the gospel of Jesus Christ has not been laid open to mankind in its original plainness, simplicity, and majesty." Or again,

> We flatter ourselves that the principles...on which the church of Christ—all believers in Jesus as the Messiah—can be united...; on which the gospel and its ordinances can be restored in all their primitive simplicity, excellency, and power...: I say, *the principles* by which these things can be done are now developed, as well as the *principles themselves*, which together constitute *the original gospel* and *order of things* established by the Apostles.[1]

Little wonder, then, that Campbell's printer published the first edition of his *Christian System* under the title, *Christianity Restored*, or that Walter Scott, Campbell's close friend and colleague, published in 1836 a very large volume he entitled, *The Gospel Restored*.[2] Scott, in fact, announced in 1827 that in eighteen centuries of Christian history, he had been the first to "restore to the world the morals—the primitive manner—of administering to mankind the gospel of our Lord Jesus Christ!"[3]

The next several years revealed a major ideological shift taking place in the ranks of Churches of Christ. Increasingly, many expressed their concern to define "the true church" in contrast to all the false churches that surrounded them. There is simply no way to overstate that this concern was something new in this tradition. The founding generation expressed no interest whatsoever in restoring the "true Church of Christ." Instead, they sought to unite all Christians on the platform of ancient Christianity. The shift that occurred in the 1830s toward a preoccupation with maintaining the "true Church of Christ," as opposed to uniting all Christians around the ancient faith, represents a virtual ideological chasm between the goals of the founding generation and the goals of those who now committed themselves to recreate and maintain the "true Church of Christ."

We find one of the most striking illustrations of this latter preoccupation in the work of a Tennessee preacher by the name of John R. Howard. In 1843, Howard published an article in his own publication, the *Bible Advocate*, threatening people with destruction if they refused to abandon their sectarian, human organizations and identify themselves with the one true church. He called upon these people

> to cast away all your unscriptural names, forms and practices; and return back to the true faith—the pure, original Gospel…The coming of the Lord, in vengeance to destroy his enemies, cannot…be very far off…And should *you* not be found among his true people—his genuine disciples— but arrayed in opposition against them, he will "destroy" you "with the *breath* of his *mouth*, and with the *brightness* of his *coming*."[4]

Five years later, Howard published a sermon that was widely circulated among members of Churches of Christ since it was reprinted in a variety of publications. As far as I can tell, this sermon represents perhaps the very first creedal statement that defined in substantial detail the beliefs and practices of what Howard called the "true Church of Christ." Ironically, item three in this seven point creed was the affirmation that "the Church now which has no creed but the *Bible*…is, all things else being equal, the true Church of Christ."[5]

Roughly contemporary with Howard, an Ohio preacher named Arthur Crihfield launched in 1837 a new gospel paper that he called, appropriately enough, the *Heretic Detector*. Crihfield apparently thought that the task of restoration had little to do with searching for truth but everything to do with exposing heretics. "Any effort to reinstate the Apostles upon their thrones, and the gospel to its honors, is an effort to detect heresy," he claimed, "since by heresy all the mischief to be repaired, has been brought about."[6] In this way, Crihfield typified a growing segment of Churches of Christ who apparently gave little thought to how they might achieve a richer and deeper understanding of gospel truths, but who devoted themselves instead to attacking their detractors and defending what they regarded as the "true Church of Christ."

The Response of the Founders

It is difficult to exaggerate the theological significance of the transition we have just described. It was a shift from a *search* for truth to the affirmation that truth had now been discovered and must be defended at all costs; and a shift from the notion of restoration as process to the notion of restoration as accomplished fact. It is little wonder, therefore, that both Alexander Campbell and Barton W. Stone rejected these claims out of hand. Stone, for example, condemned in 1836 members of Churches of Christ who sought to encompass the truth in *unwritten* creeds and then to exclude those who could not agree with that particular standard of orthodoxy.

> Some among ourselves were for some time zealously engaged to do away [with] party creeds, and are yet zealously preaching against them—but instead of a written creed of man's device, they have substituted a non-descript one, and exclude good brethren from their fellowship, because they dare believe differently from their opinions, and like other sectarians endeavor to destroy their influence in the world.[7]

Six years earlier, Stone even rebuked some followers of Alexander Campbell for their tendency to reduce the boundless truth of God to a single article of belief and a single practice. "Should they make their own peculiar view of immersion a term of fellowship," he wrote,

> it will be impossible for them to repel, successfully, the imputation of being sectarians, and of having an authoritative creed (though not written) of one article at least,

which is formed of their own opinion of truth; and this short creed would exclude more christians from union than any creed with which I am acquainted.[8]

But what about Alexander Campbell? It is undeniably true that Campbell made extravagant claims regarding the movement he led and thereby contributed to the mindset Stone rejected. At the same time, Campbell remained fundamentally unsympathetic with efforts to turn this movement into a quest to defend the "true Church of Christ." As early as 1826, for example, Campbell recognized this tendency in the movement and registered his protest in no uncertain terms.

> This plan of making our own nest, and fluttering over our own brood; of building our own tent, and of confining all goodness and grace to our noble selves and the "elect few" who are like us, is the quintessence of sublimated pharisaism…To lock ourselves up in the bandbox of our own little circle; to associate with a few units, tens, or hundreds, as the pure church, as the elect, is real Protestant monkery, it is evangelical nunnery.[9]

Twelve years later, Campbell rejected Walter Scott's audacious claim that he (Scott) had been the one who restored the gospel to the earth. "*To restore the gospel* is really a great matter," Campbell observed, "and implies that the persons who are the subjects of such a favor once had it and lost it." These were claims Campbell refused to make. In fact, he expressed his gratitude that he had never "put the title 'Christianity Restored' nor 'Gospel Restored' to any thing I ever wrote."[10]

In 1837, Campbell engaged in a crucial exchange with a woman from Lunenburg, Virginia. The woman wrote to Campbell to register her shock that Campbell "recognize[d] the Protestant parties as Christian" and found Christians "in all Protestant parties." She understood, she said, that the name Christian belonged to none "but those who believe the *gospel*, repent, and are buried by baptism into the death of Christ."

To those accustomed to the notion of the one true church, Campbell's response must have come as quite a shock. If there are no Christians among the Protestant churches, Campbell observed, then there are "no Christians in the world except ourselves"—a notion Campbell found patently ludicrous. As far as Campbell was concerned, the name Christian legitimately belonged to "every one that believes in his heart that Jesus of Nazareth is the Messiah, the Son of God; repents of his sins, and obeys him in all things according to his measure of knowledge of his will." Campbell affirmed that he could not and would not "make any one duty the standard of Christian state or character, not even immersion into the name of the Father, of the Son, and of the Holy Spirit." And then, in the most critical passage of this all-important article, Campbell wrote,

> Should I find a Pedobaptist more intelligent in the Christian Scriptures, more spiritually-minded and more devoted to the Lord than a Baptist, or one immersed on a profession of the ancient faith, I could not hesitate a moment in giving the preference of my heart to him that loveth most. Did I act otherwise, I would be a pure sectarian, a Pharisee among Christians....And should I see a sectarian Baptist or a Pedobaptist more spiritually-minded, more generally conformed to the requisitions of the Messiah, than one who precisely acquiesces with me in the theory or practice of immersion as I teach, doubtless the former rather than the latter, would have my cordial approbation and love as a Christian. So I judge, and so I feel. It is the image of Christ the Christian looks for and loves; and this does not consist in being exact in a few items, but in general devotion to the whole truth as far as known.

The fundamental assumption on which Campbell rested this entire argument was his conviction that because human beings are human and not God, they are therefore frail and fallible and may not always see things exactly alike. Accordingly, Campbell asked his readers,

> How many are there who cannot read; and of those who can read, how many are so deficient in education; and of those educated, how many are ruled by the authority of those whom they regard as superiors in knowledge and piety, that they never can escape out of the dust and smoke of their own chimney, where they happened to be born and educated!

Based on that assumption, Campbell took it for granted that many a good man has been mistaken. Mistakes are to be regarded as culpable and as declarative of a corrupt heart only when they proceed from a wilful neglect of the means of knowing what is commanded. Ignorance is always a crime when it is voluntary; and innocent when it is involuntary. Now, unless I could prove that all who neglect the positive institutions of Christ and have substituted for them something else of human authority, do it knowingly, or, if not knowingly, are voluntarily ignorant of what is written, I could not, I dare not say that their mistakes are such as unchristianize all their professions. [11]

What Was at Stake in This Dispute?

What was at stake in this dispute between Campbell and Stone, on the one hand, and some of their contemporaries, on the other? A casual examination of this exchange might lead us to imagine that it reflected nothing more than the old debates over baptism or the boundaries of Christian fellowship that have stood at the center of our movement for almost two full centuries. But the most fundamental issue involved in this dispute centered on the nature of God. Was God free to define the truth, or must God conform to our definitions and understandings? Was God free to accept into the church those whom he chose to accept, or must God bow to our decision regarding who is legitimately Christian and who is not? Was God free to save those he wished to save, or must God save only those whom we have determined are fit for his Kingdom?

To put this another way—when the founders insisted that the Christian walk is a perpetual search for truth, they implicitly affirmed their conviction that God is God, that he is All Truth and All Wisdom, that he is the Transcendent One whose ways are not our ways, and that his thoughts are beyond our thoughts as the heavens are beyond the earth. At the same time, by insisting that the Christian walk is a perpetual search for truth, the founders also affirmed that human beings are finite and fundamentally flawed, and because we inevitably possess profound and far-reaching limitations, we simply cannot comprehend the mind of God. For this reason, we have only one legitimate choice: We must let God be God.

The founders obviously believed that there is much we can know about God from the revelation he has given to us in Jesus Christ and from the God-inspired witness to that revelation which is the biblical text. At the same time, they also believed that there is much we do not know, and much that we will inevitably misunderstand and misinterpret. This is precisely why Campbell felt the need to reevaluate his own presuppositions day after day after day. In fact, Campbell never thought the day would come when there would be no need for that reevaluation process.

In other words, the founders believed the great biblical truth that God is God and that human beings are human beings, and that a great gulf exists between the two. They took seriously words like these from the prophet Isaiah:

> Who has understood the mind of the LORD, or instructed him as his counselor? (Isaiah 40:13 NIV)
>
> Do you not know?
> Have you not heard?
> The LORD is the everlasting God,
> the Creator of the ends of the earth.
> He will not grow tired or weary,
> and his understanding no man can fathom. (Isaiah 40:28, NIV)

They took seriously Isaiah's report that when he saw the Lord, "seated on a throne, high and exalted," he could only respond with those self-revealing words, "Woe to me! I am ruined! For I am a man of unclean lips, and I live among a people of unclean lips, and my eyes have seen the King, the Lord Almighty."

They took seriously God's speech to Job,

> "Who is this that darkens my counsel with words without knowledge?" (Job 38:2, NIV)

And Job's response to God,

> "You asked, 'Who is this that obscures my counsel without knowledge?'
> Surely I spoke of things I did not understand,
> things too wonderful for me to know.
> You said, 'Listen now, and I will speak;
> I will question you, and you shall answer me.'
> My ears had heard of you
> but now my eyes have seen you.
> Therefore I despise myself and repent in dust and ashes."
> (Job 42:3–6, NIV)

Alexander Campbell and Barton W. Stone surely believed the promise, "You shall know the truth and the truth shall make you free" (John 8:32). But based on everything we know about those men, they understood that the truth that would make us free was not a static set of propositions about the church or the plan of salvation or the five acts of worship or how we should organize our congregations. Rather, they knew that the truth that would set us free was the truth that God is God, that all human beings are finite and frail and fallible, and that we are therefore saved, not by our knowledge or our works or our ability finally to restore the ancient church in its every detail, but simply by virtue of God's incredible grace, offered to us in His Son, Jesus the Christ.

On the other hand, when some began to argue that truth had been recovered and the ancient church restored, and when they launched their defense of the one "true Church of Christ" in opposition to those who saw things from a different angle of vision, precisely at that point, those who made these claims compromised the most fundamental presupposition of our movement. In effect, they transformed the Stone-Campbell Movement into a profoundly humanistic movement that trusted not so much in the power of God as in the ability of self-sufficient human beings to get things right and, for all practical purposes, to save themselves. Perhaps even more important, those who made this change placed the Lord of heaven and earth in a very small box, whose walls they built of human judgment and human interpretation. The builders of the box imagined these walls were firm and secure since, from their limited angle of vision, they seemed altogether rational and fundamentally biblical. But they failed to acknowledge that the Lord of heaven and earth shatters every box in which we seek to place Him; refuses to be confined by words, even biblical words; and therefore shatters every formula, every definition, every pattern, every plan, and every form of orthodoxy we can possibly devise to contain him. Simply put, the builders of the box sought to manage a God who will not be managed.

How Did We Lose Our Way?
How Can We Find Our Way Home?

The irony in this development is unmistakable. How could those who so strongly objected to creeds and human systems have finally put God in a box? That is an interesting question, but a far more pressing question is this: How can we in our generation embrace a more biblical doctrine of God? How can we catch a fuller vision of His greatness and glory and power? And on the other side of the coin, how can we embrace a more realistic assessment of our own limitations and failures? How can we acknowledge the many ways in which our own wisdom and understanding simply fail to serve us as well as we might wish?

For all practical purposes, these questions are all one question and point to the same consistent answer, which is simply this: we must embrace the truth that we, too, are human beings. That may seem a strange thing to say since it is so obvious that this is the case. And yet, for almost two hundred years, we have sought in various ways to deny our humanness and to affirm that we are something we are not. We have done this because so often, we have confused the ideals we embrace with the reality of our present situation. For example, we have aspired for many years to restore the purity of the ancient church of Jesus Christ. That has been an ideal. But in our zeal to implement that ideal, we have sometimes allowed ourselves to believe that we have no human founders whatsoever, no history but the story of the faithful recorded in the biblical text, no theology but the Bible itself, and that, in fact, we ourselves are nothing more and nothing less than the church of the first Christian age. When we make these kinds of assumptions, we implicitly deny that we are real human beings living in real human history.

The question of our own human history is in many ways the fundamental question we must address in this regard. Once, when I was teaching at Abilene Christian University, and attending one of the largest congregations of Churches of Christ in that city, I taught a Sunday school class for junior high school students on the history of Christianity. Most of the twenty-five or thirty students in that class were children of ACU professors. We began in the beginning, with the day of Pentecost, then slowly made our way through the history of the church. We explored the early persecutions, the Apostolic Fathers, Augustine, Aquinas, Luther, Calvin, Zwingli, the Anabaptists, and the Puritans. Then, finally, the day came for the exploration of the history of our own particular movement in the United States. I thought surely some of the students would know something already about Alexander Campbell and Barton W. Stone, at the very least. After all, these children had been raised in the Church of Christ and, more than that, had lived on the ACU hill all their lives. How could they possibly avoid knowing about the heritage of our movement?

And so I began class that morning by asking the simple question, "How many of you know the name Alexander Campbell?" To my surprise, I got only fish eyes. "How many of you know the name Barton W. Stone?" Fish eyes, once again. It turned out that in that class of twenty-five or thirty students, each of them raised in the very bosom of the Churches of Christ, only one child had ever so much as heard the names Alexander Campbell and Barton W. Stone. That child was my own son, Andy.

It occurred to me that day that these students knew nothing about their own religious heritage because most of their mothers and fathers, most of the elders of the church, most of the Sunday school teachers, and most of the members thought this kind of knowledge fundamentally irrelevant. Because they sought to be New Testament Christians, not Campbellites or Stoneites, and in their zeal to claim authentic biblical faith, not some nineteenth-century version of that biblical faith, they virtually denied their own history. No wonder their children had never heard of Alexander Campbell or Barton W. Stone.

And yet, there is no possible way we can escape our history. We are, after all, human beings. We *have* been shaped in countless ways by Alexander Campbell and Barton Stone, by Tolbert Fanning and Moses Lard, by Benjamin Franklin and David Lipscomb, and by so many others whose names we may not know but who nonetheless helped define the very particular tradition in which we stand. This is why I have acknowledged throughout the course of these lectures the role played by Alexander Campbell and Barton Stone as two of the "founders" of our tradition. To make that confession in no way detracts from the fact that the ultimate founder and author of our faith is the Lord Jesus Christ.

The truth is, if we deny our history, we only become victims of the history we seek to escape. For example, if we deny that Alexander Campbell played a powerful role in shaping our most fundamental presuppositions about the Bible and the Christian faith—if we deny that fact, we may become Campbellites with a vengeance. After all, if we deny Campbell's place in our movement, there is no way to critique or assess the very real influence he has exerted on each of us. We cannot critique the ideas and presuppositions we have inherited from Campbell because, in effect, we pretend that Campbell did not exist. If we pretend that Campbell did not exist, we then cripple our ability either to affirm his positive contributions or liberate ourselves from his negative contributions. The truth is, by denying our history, we allow ourselves to become ten times more the children of Alexander Campbell than we might be if we acknowledged our history honestly, candidly, and forthrightly.

The paradox is this: Only when we acknowledge our history can we be freed from the constraints of our history. Only then are we freed to embrace or reject specific ideas or presuppositions that we have inherited from Campbell, Stone, and others who have placed their stamp on this movement. But if we deny our history, we are victims of a story we don't even know. But there is more at stake here even than this. If we deny our history, we make ourselves into something we are not. We lift ourselves from the plane of ordinary mortal existence to some transcendent realm, untouched and unaffected by human experience. In effect, we make ourselves gods. If, therefore, we wish to catch a fuller glimpse of the glory, the grandeur, and the power of God, and if we wish to embrace a more realistic assessment of our own failures and limitations, there is no better way to begin than to come to terms with our own very human history.

Closely connected with this issue is our common claim that Churches of Christ do not constitute a denomination. I want to explore that claim in the light of the larger issue of the nature and meaning of God.

In the early nineteenth century, it made a great deal of sense to claim that we were not a denomination, for in a very literal and realistic sense, we simply were not. We were a movement, designed to bring all Christians into a common orbit around the principles of the first Christian age. In those days, the claim that we were not a denomination served a descriptive purpose, not a theological purpose.

In time, however, we ceased to be a movement and became a very particular organization. We had "our" churches and "our" papers, "our" lectureships and "our" preachers, "our" colleges and "our" people. Clearly, we no longer comprised a loosely constructed movement. Instead, we had become a well-defined religious organization alongside other religious organizations. Yet, we continued to claim that we were not a denomination.

What could that claim have possibly meant in that context? We must acknowledge that by the mid-nineteenth century, to claim that the Church of Christ was not a denomination was to make a theological statement, not a purely descriptive statement. In time, this claim became a theological shibboleth, an assumption that carried with it a considerable amount of theological freight. Listen, for example, to John Rogers who argued in 1860 that members of Churches of Christ should never speak of the "other denominations." "When we speak of other *denominations*," Rogers wrote, "we place ourselves *among them*, as one of *them*. This, however, we can never do, unless we abandon the distinctive ground—the apostolic ground—the antisectarian ground, we have taken."[12]

Clearly, the nondenominational language was simply another way of underscoring our contention that while other churches floundered in history and tradition, we were the one true church since we had found the truth and restored the church, just as it existed in the first Christian age. Presumably, we, too, would become a denomination if we were to compromise biblical truth in the slightest degree. Our nondenominational status, therefore, depended on our ability to remain faithful to the apostolic ground on which we had staked our claim.

Paul underscores the theological problem with this kind of claim in Galatians 3:10: "All who rely on observing the law are under a curse, for it is written: 'Cursed is everyone who does not continue to do everything written in the Book of the Law'" (NIV). If we extrapolate from Paul's statement a meaning appropriate to our own situation in the nineteenth century, we might argue that we were under obligation to restore the ancient church in every detail, lest we become a denomination and thereby fall under judgment.

But beyond the claim that we had fully restored the ancient church, the nondenominational language carried with it other fundamental and far-reaching assumptions. Implicitly it suggested that Churches of Christ were immune to the power of history and culture and tradition. Other religious organizations fell prey to these inexorable forces, but we did not. Other religious organizations had their vision clouded by ordinary human limitations, but we did not. Somehow, we had burst the bounds of our human constraints to achieve a perfection denied to everyone else. In effect, then, we refused to confess the depths of our own humanity, the first step toward confessing that God alone is the living God.

Surely, it is legitimate to claim that the denominational arrangement is wrong, since we know full well that Jesus prayed for the unity of all believers. But why must we claim that we do not partake of that sin? In what other areas of our lives do we claim to be sinless? What possible purpose is served when we claim perfection in this regard?

Suppose we refused to root our self-understanding in the righteousness we achieve by faithfully restoring the ancient church. Suppose, instead, we rooted our self-understanding in the righteousness whereby God makes us righteousness, in spite of our faults and, indeed, in spite of our failure to faithfully reproduce the ancient church? If we took the righteousness of God as our starting point, would it not then make sense to make the more modest claim that because the denominational arrangement is wrong, we therefore reject it in principle? But would it not also make sense to confess that we may well partake of that sin along with everyone else? To make that confession is not to state that we willfully violate the unity of the body of Christ. Rather, to make that confession is to acknowledge that we are finite human beings, inevitably bound to certain historical and cultural structures from which we cannot extricate ourselves. One of those structures is the denominational arrangement in the United States.

Frankly, I have felt for many years that our nondenominational claims carry with them such an affirmation of perfection and such a denial of our humanity and our finitude that they effectively block us from two of the greatest gifts of the Christian faith. One such gift is the search for truth that is surely our birthright, not only as participants in the Stone-Campbell tradition, but also as members in the body of Christ. But how can we possibly keep alive a meaningful search for truth if we claim that we are not a denomination, but rather the "true Church of Christ," now restored in its fullness to the earth. The other gift is the greatest gift of all, the gift of God's grace, which is the Gospel of Jesus Christ. But how can we possibly hear the gospel if we are preoccupied with our own perfection?

Conclusions

My purpose in these two lectures has been to highlight what I take to be one of the central themes in the Stone-Campbell tradition in the early years of our movement, namely, the notion that God is God and all human beings are fallible. Alexander Campbell and Barton Stone seldom made direct and explicit statements to that effect, but they pointed unmistakably to their convictions in that regard when they spoke about truth. On the one hand, they insisted that every human being has the God-given right to search for truth. On the other, they argued that no one can possibly capture the truth, possess the truth, or codify the truth. They made these points time and again, simply because they knew that God is truth and the source of truth, and that human beings can never capture the truth of God in a creed or a system or a plan or an orthodoxy of any form, shape, or fashion.

I also argued that reforming movements dedicated to a larger vision of the truth of God often lose sight of that original goal within a few generations. This was surely the case with Lutherans, Calvinists, and Anabaptists in the sixteenth century. In Churches of Christ, however, this transformation occurred within a few short years. While Campbell and Stone had pressed for a perpetual search for truth, some in Churches of Christ now claimed that the truth was now found and the search was therefore closed. And while Campbell and Stone claimed that God's truth defies consummation and that restoration must therefore be an ongoing process, some among Churches of Christ began to claim that restoration was now complete. My contention is that those who made these claims subverted the very essence of the Stone-Campbell tradition.

I love this tradition and I want to see it flourish. But I am convinced that it will flourish again only when we take seriously the fact that ours is a finite movement and not the fullness of the kingdom of God. I am convinced that it will flourish again only when we extend to every person the unalienable right to search for truth. I am convinced that it will flourish again only when we proclaim in all our congregations the lordship of Jesus Christ and the sovereignty of Almighty God. And I am convinced that it will flourish again when we fall on our knees and confess our failures not only as individual Christians but also as a community of believers who wear the name, "the Churches of Christ." Our ability to make that confession is rooted deeply in the Stone-Campbell tradition. As John Rogers put it many years ago, "we have no reason to conclude, we know all the truth....We have nothing to lose in this inquiry after truth. We have no system to bind us to human opinions." May we take that confession seriously as we prepare to proclaim the kingdom of God in the coming millennium.

NOTES

[1]Alexander Campbell, *The Christian System*, 5th ed. (1835; reprint, Cincinnati: Standard Publishing, 1901), 154, xi–xii.

[2]Walter Scott, *The Gospel Restored: A Discourse* (Cincinnati, 1836).

[3]Walter Scott, "From the Minutes of the Mahoning Association Report," *Christian Examiner* 1 (November 1829), 5–8.

[4]Howard, "A Warning to the Religious Sects and Parties in Christendom," *Bible Advocate* 1 (January 1843), 82.

[5]John R. Howard, "The Beginning Corner; or, The Church of Christ Identified," *American Christian Review* 1 (August 1856), 226–35. This sermon was first published under the title, "Identification of the Church of Christ" in Tolbert Fanning's *Christian Magazine* 1 (September 1848), 267ff.

[6]Arthur Crihfield, "To T. M. Henley," *Heretic Detector* 1 (15 May 1837), 132.

[7]Barton W. Stone, "Desultory Remarks," *Christian Messenger* 10 (December 1836), 182.

[8]Stone, n.t., *Christian Messenger* 4 (August 1830), 201.

[9]Campbell, "To an Independent Baptist," *Christian Baptist* 3 (May 1, 1826), 204.

[10]Campbell, "Events of 1823 and 1827," *Millennial Harbinger*, New Series, 2 (October 1838), 466.

[11]Campbell, "Any Christians Among Protestant Parties," *Millennial Harbinger*, New Series, 1 (September 1837), 411–13.

[12]John Rogers, *A Discourse Delivered in Carlisle, Kentucky,1860* (Cincinnati, 1861), 22.

CHAPTER 5

Keeping the "Current Reformation" Current

The Challenge of Ongoing Self-interpretation in the Stone-Campbell Tradition

Paul M. Blowers

It seems quite natural, as the Stone-Campbell Movement approaches not only the new millennium but also the various celebrations which will mark its own bicentennial, that there has been increased interest in reevaluating the movement's past achievements, appraising its present status in ecumenical Christianity, and making projections about the peculiar challenges that its bearers will face in a new century. The Forrest-Kirkpatrick Seminars hosted by the Disciples of Christ Historical Society addressed, from 1994 to 1996, the general theme of "A Nineteenth-Century Religious Movement Faces the Twenty-First Century."[1] And now too the Society's Reed Lectures for 1995 and 1997 have taken up the theme of "Founding Vocation and Future Vision" as it bespeaks the challenges of ongoing self-definition and self-understanding particularly in the Christian Church (Disciples of Christ) and the Churches of Christ.[2]

This kind of assessment of where we have been in the venerable past, where we stand in the opportune present, and where we might be or should be headed in the uncertain future was likewise a preoccupation of Disciples around the turn of the twentieth century when, for example, J. H. Garrison edited a volume of essays by various authors entitled *The Reformation of the Nineteenth Century*,[3] and shortly thereafter composed his own narrative, *The Story of a Century*, published in 1909, the year of the Disciples of Christ Centennial. Turning from past achievements to the obstacles and unfinished tasks ahead, Garrison remarked:

> When any religious movement reaches the conclusion that it has mastered all truth and has accomplished the work it was intended to accomplish, its mission, of course, is ended. Happily no such feeling exists, at least among the representative men of this current Reformation. It is destined always to remain a *current* and not a *past* Reformation. Its principles make this a necessity.[4]

> Openmindedness to the truth, the willingness to receive new truth, the humility that recognizes the limitations of our knowledge, the eagerness to know all that God would teach us—this is the remedy for all our imperfections and errors in judgment, as it is the prophecy of an ever-brightening career of usefulness for any man or movement striving to reach the higher ideals. A continuous reformation, adjusting itself to the varying conditions and needs of the world, ours must be, or it must decay and cease to be a Reformation at all, becoming a monument rather than a movement.[5]

Our Reed Lecturers, Anthony Dunnavant and Richard Hughes, clearly share Garrison's premise, and both seem to concur that one of the prerequisites for keeping the "Current Reformation" current is the need for disciplined, ongoing self-interpretation, for critical reflection on our core principles and their adaptability amid the constantly changing landscape of American, and indeed *world*, Christianity.

As I see it, these lectures shed light on three crucial issues lying at the heart of this continuing process of interpreting, and in a certain constructive sense "reinventing," ourselves: (1) the root problem of *identifying or locating the "founding vocation"* of the Stone-Campbell Movement as conceived and articulated by its first-generation leaders; (2) the challenge of *appropriating the core principles* of the movement, translating them from a nineteenth-century context in which a foundationalist, bibliocentric Protestant worldview dominated American culture to a culture at the turn of the twenty-first century that appears increasingly nonfoundationalist and conducive to multiple rival worldviews; and (3) the specific *process of discernment* whereby we seek to understand our identity and role in the current global spectrum of Christianity, and cast a "future vision" reflecting a renewed vocation in the life and mission of the Church catholic.

Identifying the "Founding Vocation"

Whoever has closely studied the early decades of the Stone-Campbell Movement is well aware that the "founders" did not at every point see eye to eye on the thrust or mission of their emerging movement. Even a theme seemingly as unifying as Christian unity admitted of variant perspectives from among Barton Stone, the Campbells, Walter Scott, and other early standard-bearers.[6] And even with individual leaders, there was a tendency over the span of a career to send some mixed signals on given issues, reflecting both the highly charged polemical atmosphere in which these leaders labored and their genuine desire to adapt, refine, or revise their views.[7] Can we nonetheless locate a core principle or motive, or perhaps a set of core principles or motives, consistently shared among the movement's originators? To put it another way, was there such a thing as *the* founding vocation of the Stone-Campbell Movement?

Dunnavant and Hughes differ significantly in their basic approaches to identifying such a "core" or "essence," even though certain of their observations harmonize. Both acknowledge the classic interpretation that has given prominence to the dual leitmotifs of "unity" and "restoration" (or unity-through-restoration); and both see these as inadequate by themselves to capture the founding vocation in its fullness. Both, moreover, respectively insist on *freedom* as a constitutive first principle of the movement. Dunnavant, however, chooses to focus on a wider set of core commitments—*freedom, apostolicity, unity, and evangelism (mission)*[8]—espoused more or less consistently among the founders and held together within a providential worldview. Out of this chemistry multiple "vectors" emerged, indicating different thrusts, and so too inaugurating different trajectories in which the movement has been carried on or traditioned by its representatives in later generations. One such vector, which Dunnavant admits as perhaps more exceptional than typical in the founders' thinking, was a certain catholic impulse, an openness to the labors of other Christian groups[9] and to a "providential" vocation larger than the Stone-Campbell Movement, in which this movement could nonetheless play a vital role. Accordingly, this catholic ethos and vocation fully flowered in the subsequent ecumenical commitments of the Disciple mainline in the twentieth century, culminating in Restructure as the organizational embodiment of this revised vocation.

Hughes, by contrast, claims to identify a singular first principle, an "essence" in the stricter ideological sense, an original "genius" that was definitive of the movement and which, while expressed by different individual leaders, effectively transcended the work of any single one. For Hughes, the Stone-Campbell Movement was essentially a *freedom* movement devoted to the *unencumbered search for truth*[10] which, while oriented toward the steadfast "platform" of primitive Christianity, grounded itself even more deeply in *the axiom that God is God, that human beings are fallible seekers after his truth, and that no human system can therefore claim finally to have "boxed in" that truth.* The "founding vocation" was the search for God's truth as an ongoing process, such that the task of restoring New Testament Christianity could never be claimed as a fait accompli.

In raising questions not only of vocation but of self-definition in the Stone-Campbell Movement, the respective approaches of Dunnavant and Hughes are in my view interestingly reminiscent of the divergent approaches in New Testament studies to the self-definition process in the earliest Christian "movement" itself. Especially influential in recent decades has been the trajectory-critical approach,[11] which has highlighted the diversity of currents or traditions in earliest Christianity, the fact that primitive communities differed significantly in their Christologies, their attachments to the mother faith of Judaism, and so on. But in the nineteenth and early twentieth centuries, particularly through the influence of Liberal Protestant historians like Adolf von Harnack,[12] the strong tendency of some was to speak of a singular "essence" (*das Wesen*) of Christianity, the simple gospel of Jesus, from which the Greek and Latin churches eventually lapsed, be it into hellenizing, dogmatizing, traditionalizing, or imperializing the original genius of the faith. The Stone-Campbell Movement represents a much less complex case study by comparison, and yet the historical dynamic is analogous. Once again we are back to the question:

Was the founding vocation of the Stone-Campbell Movement an evolving combination of different impulses or thrusts (thus leading to different representative traditions), or was it based on a perspicuous first principle, a truly original and definitive "genius" or "essence"?

Dunnavant's own "vector" or "trajectory" approach to the Stone-Campbell Movement has the strength of accounting for the diversity, fluidity, and dynamism of strategy operative in the formative years, the varied commitments taking shape simultaneously in and among the founders, the dissonance that occasionally appears among them, and their potential to inspire divergent interpretive legacies. Stone, the Campbells, Scott, and other early leaders did not, it seems, collectively isolate one definitive leitmotif to comprehend their labors. It was a wide-ranging, providential, and indeed *millennial* project. Within it, liberation, restoration, unity and evangelistic mission belonged to the same agenda, to be sure, but they did not fall together mechanically as component parts of some transcendent "movement" model. At most there was a viable consensus, a reasonably consistent configuration of emphases: unity through restoration (apostolic integrity) for the sake of world evangelization.[13] Inevitably there were constituents who would seize upon one particular vocation (say, restoration as opposed to unity) as more crucial and definitive than any other, particularly as the movement grew rapidly and the stakes of its self-definition became ever higher. Out of the full gamut of the movement's incipient commitments, this could only be expected. But the founding vocation was never fixed in an ideological vacuum, any more than "New Testament Christianity," as Thomas Campbell insisted, was sealed up in a purely theoretical vacuum.[14]

Those who want to define the Stone-Campbell Movement strictly as a *restoration* movement are bound to find Dunnavant's "vector" approach unsatisfactory precisely because it does not locate a final touchstone of *normative* self-definition within the movement's early history to which all who identify with it would in principle have to be held accountable. The thread that holds the movement's basic commitments together is not any singularly privileged commitment or principle, but instead the overarching "providential worldview," the openness to participating in a divine work larger than all the particularities of the denominations. Devout restorationists, however, will doubtless see this as far too vague and as failing to settle on *the* founding vocation in terms that could provide a clear-cut agenda for calling the different branches of the movement back to the "original" mission. They will want to point again to the self-assurance of the early leadership that theirs was a biblically warranted mission to recover and sustain the New Testament "constitution" of the Church amid the din of sectarian rivalries.

Hughes's approach appears prima facie to answer the ostensible need for a more definitive expression of the Stone-Campbell movement's founding vocation. He presupposes that while restoration was properly basic to the movement's agenda, there was an even more profound "genius" or "essence," definitive of what this restoration movement *is*, namely, the *heuristic* principle of free and perpetual striving after God's truth, conditioned by the humble recognition that God is always greater than our limited human efforts at restoration. This is the essence of the movement, and yet virtually from the beginning there was a falling away from this genius, just as the Lutheran, Reformed, and Anabaptist movements fell away from their essential selves. It is a familiar Protestant historiographical logic. Dogmatism, sterile institutionalization, or in our case restorationist exclusivism have led the various churches down a stray path, and the animating dynamic is to recover the original genius of the founders.

Hughes's reconstruction is compelling, but in my view flawed in its historical claim that the heuristic principle itself was the true bottom line. What we have, at most, is evidence that at crucial points in the Stone-Campbell movement's early development and growth, the early leaders, while encouraging the free investigation of the truth, held in check a pernicious self-centeredness or pretension to have owned that truth. No doubt this warning is important to our identity as a movement. Indeed there is even more evidence of this timely humility than Hughes or Dunnavant had the time to detail in their lectures. I am reminded, for example, of the last (yet in some respects most consequential) of Alexander Campbell's rules for biblical interpretation, which imposes a healthy caution on the hermeneutics of restoration. After all the proper science has been done, the scrupulous application of the grammatical-historical method been carried out, the Christian interpreter (and thus too the church as interpreting community) is constrained to have the "moral soundness of vision," the disciplined humility, and the godly docility to listen for the voice of God.[15] No room for arrogance here. And yet this timely humility must itself be put in proper perspective. In the same rules of interpretation Campbell clearly presumes confidence in the dignified abilities of native human intelligence for the hermeneutical task, and sets out "nature" and "revelation" as "twin sisters of the same divine parentage."[16] We are a far cry here from the kind of deep embrace of divine sovereignty and human disability which, as Douglas Foster pointed out in his oral response to Hughes's lectures, evokes more an axiom of Reformed theology than a driving ideal of the Stone-Campbell Movement.[17] Whatever their Presbyterian roots, the founders were on their guard against the implications of such a conviction, which in their view could actually militate against the freedom to pursue scriptural truth. As Robert Richardson wrote in 1848, "The popular views respecting the exercise of the divine sovereignty, and concerning human depravity and incapacity, have induced men to suppose a direct interposition of divine power necessary to enable any one to understand the word of God."[18]

My own sense, overall, is that the need to determine the exact parameters of the "founding vocation" is more a problem for *us* than it was for the founders themselves. Certainly they had their core commitments: an unambiguous devotion to the cause of Christian unity, an equally unambiguous devotion to restoring the authority of the New Testament, and yet another unambiguous devotion to evangelizing the world. These are so conscientiously and candidly set out in the literature that we can affirm them as properly basic to this movement. But the founders themselves trusted in the New Testament as their charter and "constitution," and in sanctified reason as their guide, and so lived happily without a systematic design for addressing every coming crisis of identity, organization, and mission. Even documents as formative and influential as the *Declaration and Address* or the younger Campbell's series on "The Restoration of the Ancient Order of Things" did more to inspire and clarify the movement's vocation than purely and simply to exhaust it.

Meanwhile Stone, the Campbells, and the rest were already "reinventing" the movement as they went along, at least in the sense of dealing on the scene with the constantly unfolding ramifications of the commitments they made, and finding their way through controversies that they at once defined and were defined by. How else can we explain, for example, the rapid creation and dismantling of the Washington Association and the Springfield Presbytery, or Alexander Campbell's "evolving" views on missionary societies, or other such signs that the movement's vocation was refined by experience? Movements, religious reformations in particular, thrive on their own dynamism, on the give-and-take within their leaderships, on their stubborn refusal to domesticate themselves, and on their ability constantly, sometimes even experimentally, to adapt themselves to changing contexts and horizons, albeit without losing their integrity.

Appropriating the Founding Vocation for Changing Times and Contexts

Besides giving perspective to the problem of identifying the founding vocation of the Stone-Campbell Movement, the Reed Lectures of Anthony Dunnavant and Richard Hughes have provided much insight into the process of self-interpretation, and the appropriation of the founding vocation for new times and contexts, in the movement's history. Here I would like to add some general observations about the cultural shifts that have impacted this process of self-interpretation, and highlight some examples of the peculiar struggles that earlier generations have faced in appropriating and adapting the movement's core commitments.

The early Stone-Campbell Movement reaped the benefits of what Henry May has called the "Didactic Enlightenment,"[19] that phase of the Enlightenment dominated by Scottish Common Sense philosophy's campaign to stifle skepticism of divine revelation and to claim the legacy of the "new science" in vindicating *Christian* truth. George Marsden has further described in detail the American cultural consensus operative in this same period of the nineteenth century, in which a bibliocentric Common Sense worldview prevailed: God was the Author of both nature and revelation, and so natural science and biblical science (the inductive method of interpretation) would mutually work to verify the self-evident, immutable, and utterly objective truths of God's good order.[20] Presbyterians, Baptists, Methodists, and Disciples alike thrived on this strongly foundationalist understanding of truth, on the epistemological confidence that Common Sense warranted, and on the seemingly boundless frontiers of "applied Christianity" open to evangelicals in a nation free of political tyranny and ecclesiastical establishments.

For our purposes, it is crucial to keep in mind that the core commitments of the Stone-Campbell Movement's founding vocation identified by Dunnavant and Hughes (viz., freedom, unity, restoration, evangelization) were originally developed in the context of the evangelical cultural consensus and with the aid of the Common Sense hermeneutic (i.e., the alliance of Common Sense philosophical realism, the Baconian-Newtonian scientific method, and Lockean epistemology). Dunnavant rightly calls this the founders' "world-taken-for-granted." By today's theological standards, in fact, the founders appear to have been thoroughgoing foundationalists. Philosophically, they presupposed the *givenness* of truth and of the fact that nature and scripture already testified to a coherent and benevolent order that could be accessed through unprejudiced investigation. This a priori philosophical confidence was matched by an overwhelming confidence in the integrity and perspicuity of the "Bible facts" as the groundwork for Christian unity and Christian mission. Thomas Campbell called all the sects to unite "upon the solid basis of universally acknowledged and self-evident truths."[21] In principle at least, there should be no mistaking the agenda set out for the churches in scripture; the elder Campbell even determined to throw out "the trite indefinite distinction between essentials and non-essentials" since the scriptural program for unity and restoration was already self-evidently laid out for everyone to see.[22]

Subsequent developments in the Stone-Campbell Movement certainly indicate, however, that the movement's biblical mandates required interpretation, nuancing, and refining of perspective. Given the confidence in the perspicuity of scripture generated by the Common Sense hermeneutic,[23] it is no surprise that some came to view the restoration of New Testament Christianity as a matter of mechanical reduplication rather than as a process of discernment and adaptation, or a matter of always witnessing *to* the New Testament churches rather than witnessing *with* the New Testament churches to the authority of Christ.[24] Robert Richardson had already expressed concerns about the direction, the depth, and the spiritual vitality of the movement[25] when, in 1856, he entered into a highly charged confrontation with Tolbert Fanning. This exchange ranged over a number of issues of philosophy and hermeneutics, but at stake was no less than the whole restoration agenda, which Richardson sensed was drifting toward a rationalistic dead end. While seeing the goal of restoring apostolic Christianity as a non-negotiable, he had genuine concerns that some (in the Fanning camp) were looking merely to "proselytize" people to the pattern of the ancient order instead of "converting" them to the ancient faith.[26] Richardson sympathized with the Common Sense hermeneutic, but he blasted Fanning who, in the name of a purely scientific interpretation of the Bible, slavishly (if unconsciously) depended on the "sensualist" (empiricist) philosophy of John Locke, which threatened to reduce interpretation merely to the gleaning of data, and to make of the Bible itself "either a rubric which prescribes forms and ordinances, or a species of mere logical machinery, independent and self-moved, to which the eternal destinies of mankind are exclusively committed."[27] The "genius" of Fanning's philosophy, Richardson noted with sarcasm, was "to resolve, as far as possible, every thing into words, propositions, arguments, and to reduce all spiritual phenomena to the forms of the ordinary understanding."[28] The Bible was thus rendered so thoroughly transparent[29] that its "facts" themselves became "the ultimate object and terminus of the Christian faith" even though scripture itself defined faith as belief in the *person* of Jesus Christ.[30]

Richardson concluded that true restoration must not lead to a "cold and heartless nominalism" and "Bibliolatry" (a term made famous by Samuel Taylor Coleridge), but must be a continuing growth in the discernment of scripture's spiritual riches, a venture of discipleship and obedience to Christ, individually and ecclesially.[31] Richardson's presupposition was that the Spirit of God was alive and well and indwelling the Church, leading the Bride of Christ toward perfection. Restoration, in this perspective, was therefore an unfinished eschatological process that had begun with the New Testament churches themselves. As Richardson put it, the "present reformation" could never stop with the restoration of the "letter" of apostolic Christianity; it needed to strive after the *whole gospel* and the fullness of the renewing power of the Holy Spirit in the life of the Church.[32]

In retrospect, the Fanning-Richardson controversy was a watershed. I mention it here because it is a prime example of how the early-generation leaders of the movement themselves sought to retain the integrity of their commitments while interpreting and adapting them to the times. Even on the dynamic American frontier (which was as much an ideological as a geographic construct[33]), the restoration agenda could easily become domesticated, drifting into a kind of biblicism and primitivism well-suited to trans-Appalachian culture but ultimately unfaithful to the New Testament's eschatological goals for the Church.

Appropriating and contextualizing the movement's vocation amid changing times and contexts have, of course, proven challenging to every new generation in the Stone-Campbell heritage.

Disciples in the late nineteenth and early twentieth centuries witnessed a cultural shift that helped foster deep division within some Protestant denominations at the same time that it ushered in an era of unprecedented denominational cooperation. Numerous factors, the upheaval of a Civil War, social change and diversification, the growth and increasing autonomy of the natural sciences, the burgeoning of biblical higher criticism and liberal theology, ultimately precipitated the demise of the evangelical cultural consensus described earlier.[34] Scores of conservatives and fundamentalists reacted by fighting to protect the Common Sense hermeneutic and clinging to the "plain" and "immutable" truths of the Bible. For progressives, however, it signaled the dawn of a new worldview. Anthony Dunnavant has magnificently traced in his second lecture the way in which some Disciples organizers, roughly in the period from the 1870s to the 1920s, seized the opportunity to liberate themselves from the old "plea," with some even willing to forfeit the restoration agenda in order to give priority to ecumenical unity and to the redefinition of Disciples ecclesiology and mission.[35]

In this period, many Disciples moderates were put in the dilemma of trying to retain the integrity of the movement's founding vocation, with its presupposition of fixed biblical truths and an "ancient order" to be restored, while adjusting that vocation to a new worldview that emphasized the organic and evolutionary nature of truth. The dilemma is interestingly hinted at in a sermon by Harvey Everest (d.1900), onetime president of Butler University, which was preached in the late nineteenth century and reprinted several years later by Z. T. Sweeney in his anthology of *New Testament Christianity*. Based on Ephesians 1:9–10 (the mystery of God's economy unfolded in the "fullness of time"), Everest's sermon extolled the divine plan in history wherein all the centuries were but a preparation for the twentieth.[36] Under divine providence, the order of nature had seen a progressive amelioration, as had the history of civilization. The Christian revelation itself, he said, was an "evolution," albeit a *finished* evolution of religion; the Bible was a completed whole, its fixed truths henceforth adaptable to all times and places.[37] Looking ahead to the twentieth century, then, Everest mused on the full millennial victory of (Protestant) Christianity coinciding with the evolutionary consummation of nature and human civilization. "The whole world of mankind is gradually approaching the kingdom of heaven, in morals, in social customs, in business honesty, in just laws, in hate of wrong, in benevolence, in Christian brotherhood."[38] This promising state of affairs was destined to be a vindication of the timeless principles of biblical Christianity, and, of course, a fulfillment of the vocation of the Stone-Campbell Movement (in particular, needless to say, a fulfillment of Alexander Campbell's own postmillennial vision).

The paradigm shift underway from a Common Sense/Baconian worldview to an evolutionary one is clearly in evidence here. Everest wanted to straddle the two, assured as he was both of the absolute immutability of divine truth on the one hand, and of the absolute (yet progress-oriented) mutability of nature and history on the other. Everest still believed in *foundations*, and in the certain millennial outcome of history, but his historical sensitivities and openness to a novel worldview trained him to the profound reality of change in the world and in culture, and therefore to the exigencies of adaptability. The yet unanticipated problem here, however, was an extraordinary overconfidence about the convergence of natural evolution, history, biblical revelation, divine providence, and the Stone-Campbell Movement. If a restorationist *primitivism* allied with Common Sense rationalism had threatened to sidetrack the Stone-Campbell Movement in the generation of Richardson and Fanning, the next two generations faced a new religio-cultural challenge: the ideological rapprochement between Protestant postmillennial optimism and a genuinely secular *progressivism* and *modernism*. Within the so-called Progressive Era, and all the more so after the breach with the Churches of Christ had been consummated, the question was whether the Disciple leadership could align the vocation of the Stone-Campbell Movement with the larger kingdom-building enterprises of federated Protestantism without losing the movement's prophetic soul. Could it embrace a providential vocation larger than the movement (as described by Dunnavant) without compromising the movement's unique witness?

In the Disciples' centennial year, J. H. Garrison certainly believed so and saw the movement at an exhilarating crossroads. And like Everest before him, he expressed profound optimism about the signs of the times. For Garrison the Disciples were no mere bystanders to the world crusade for Christian unity; they were already helping to engineer it. In his own words, "the Campbellian reformation of the nineteenth century" was now in the twentieth century destined to be appreciably better represented in the bodies of evangelical Protestantism; it was already a "permeating influence" in the religious thought and life of the times. Sectarianism and walls of separation were tumbling down, a spirit of transdenominational fraternity arising; and thus in 1909

> all thoughtful men seem to recognize the fact that [the church] is now in a transition state, passing from the older Protestantism of mutual antagonisms to the newer catholicism, in which both liberty and unity are to be conserved, and Christian fellowship shall be coextensive with Christian discipleship. . . .Christ is coming to his own in these last days.[39]

Looking back over the twentieth century, Garrison's optimism of course appears to have been quite premature. The Disciples were headed for remarkable achievements in the ecumenical movement and on other fronts, but just ahead, especially from the 1920s on, were substantial disputes within their own ranks, ideological and organizational controversies that betrayed enduring internal differences of interpretation over the vocation and direction of the Stone-Campbell Movement. Disciples progressives cast their lot with the "Protestant Establishment" and the Christian Church (Disciples of Christ) has experienced the fortunes and misfortunes of that mainline alignment.[40] Emerging "independents" pursued a restoration agenda that was rarely open to the larger providential work of God in ecumenical Christianity, such that the Christian Churches/Churches of Christ, historically, have tended to divorce their commitments to restoration and evangelism from a sustained commitment to Christian unity.[41] In the same period too, as Richard Hughes has demonstrated, Churches of Christ have had to deal with their own dilemma of a paradoxically "denominational" sectarianism.[42]

For our purposes, however, these historical ironies should not be allowed to detract from the achievement of J. H. Garrison and others of his generation who were seeking to help the movement find its way into a whole new urban and global frontier in the twentieth century. For he, like Robert Richardson, Isaac Errett, and other prophetic figures at key turning points in the movement's history, saw it as a matter of conscience and of faithfulness to the founding vocation itself to continue to take risks and to focus on a future vision in which the movement owned its core commitments precisely by adapting and contextualizing them. Garrison's perspective at the time of the movement's centennial is still prophetic:

> "We know in part, and we prophesy in part." There are many great and vital parts of God's Word which we apprehend as yet only vaguely, and many of the old truths which are familiar to us are destined to assume new meanings, and new value as we grow up to a clearer and deeper apprehension of them. There is no perfect theology.
>
> We must "follow on to know the Lord." We must not close our eyes nor our hearts to the new truths which he may show us, nor to the new and more satisfactory views of old truths which come with our enlarged Christian experience. This progress in knowledge of truth will involve a change of emphasis which we must not fail to make if we are to keep step with the great providential movements of God in the world.[43]

Identity, Discernment, and the "Future Vision" of the Stone-Campbell Movement

Whether we say, at the end of the twentieth century, that we live in radical modernity or else, as seems more likely, in nascent postmodernity, it is hard to deny that yet another paradigm shift begs to impose itself on the constituencies of the Stone-Campbell Movement, one that has thrown into question any overconfidence in an epistemically stable, identifiably *objective* body of truth, biblical or otherwise. Nonfoundationalism, both as a philosophical critique of "modern" epistemological assumptions and, in the register of theology, as a wide-ranging reorientation to the "contextuality, contingency, and revisability of knowledge,"[44] has profoundly affected the religious culture in which most Western Christians live. We are having to become increasingly trained to the reality of dealing "fairly" with pluralism and difference of perspective. We are having to be more rigorously self-conscious about the ways in which, as religious communities, we authorize our truth claims. As Christian communities, whether we like it or not in the postmodern setting, we are increasingly being challenged to understand religious truth less in terms of the metaphysical or logical structures that *define* our belief system, and more in terms of the communal language and communal narratives that enable us to *describe* who we are and what we are seeking to do in the world.[45]

Needless to say, postmodernity poses a whole new set of challenges to a movement that originally grounded its vocation and its vision in the divine *order* of revelation, a movement that invested much in the "self-evident truths" of the Bible, in the power of highly disciplined inferential reasoning, and in the conviction that all factions and denominations could unite on certain core principles as incontestably basic and ultimately immune to confusion with "human opinions." The work of processing the shift into postmodernity and interpreting our vocation for the twenty-first century is already well underway among the three major branches of the Stone-Campbell heritage, evidenced by an accumulating literature of self-interpretation and prognostication.[46] Each branch in its own way is expressing a certain identity crisis, not only as concerns postmodern culture but in relation to the dramatic reconfiguration in American religious life that has transpired over the last three decades.[47]

In this connection, I greatly value the way that Dunnavant and Hughes, in their Reed Lectures, have urged us to look, critically but constructively, to the instincts of our own heritage when dealing with issues of self-understanding and adaptability. They have focused us on some of the core commitments of the movement (freedom, restoration [apostolicity], unity, evangelism); but they have also focused us on learned virtues such as theological humility and openness to the providential working of God. While we could continue indefinitely to discuss whether any one of these commitments or virtues was definitive of, or even included within, the founding vocation of the movement, one can scarcely deny that they are all imperative for the future vision of the movement.

At the close of his second lecture, Anthony Dunnavant speaks of another virtue, *discernment*, as a priority for the Christian Church (Disciples of Christ) in its continuing attempts to deal with controversial issues among its constituent churches.[48] In my estimation, discernment may just be the great lost Christian virtue, desperately needed for all the churches of the Stone-Campbell tradition in shaping a future vision for the next century. Robert Richardson already said it best back in 1856: "It is this want of spiritual discernment and of true faith, which, in every age of Christianity, has proved an insurmountable obstacle to the reception and full comprehension of Divine truth."[49] Discernment (*diakrisis*) is of course listed by Paul among the spiritual gifts (1 Cor. 12:8–9), and yet he clearly considers it more than an individual charism; it is an *ecclesial* virtue, closely connected with discretion and intended for exercise by the whole of the gathered Christian community (cf. Rom. 12:2; 1 Cor. 14:29; 1 Thess. 5:20–21). The aspect of discernment as a *grace* needs to be emphasized as well, since it is more than an ability or aptitude. The prolific fifth-century spiritual writer John Cassian, who celebrated discernment as the root of all the other Christian virtues, said it well: "This is no minor virtue, nor one which can be seized anywhere merely by human effort. It is ours only as a gift from God and we read in the apostle that it is to be numbered among the most outstanding gifts of the Holy Spirit."[50]

Discernment is a crucial gift to the church for the eschatological meantime in which we do not yet see perfectly, but only "in a mirror dimly" (1 Cor. 13:12); and thus it speaks quite meaningfully to the church's witness in a postmodern world that is highly suspicious of the claim that any religious truth is already "self-evident." As Luke Timothy Johnson recommends in his excellent book *Scripture and Discernment*, discernment in its properly ecclesial dimension is a gift that enables the church, congregationally and universally, to sustain its Christian identity while meeting new challenges to its identity in the world. It is the exercise of sound judgment in making decisions that will critically affect the future life of the church, and thus presupposes a *process* incorporating the whole life of the church. Necessarily it will require careful theological interpretation of canonical scripture, the use of confessional narratives, the focus provided by worship or liturgy, and the critical canvassing of issues and problems in the churches' present experience. The goal of this process of discernment is a sanctified consensus in which the will of God is determined and acted upon that may possibly entail much controversy before it can be achieved.[51]

A number of Johnson's recommendations concerning the discernment process are especially appropriate to the churches of the Stone-Campbell tradition as they "reinvent" themselves for a new century. First, our discernment will require careful scrutiny of the way we base our self-understanding and our vocation on the Bible itself. *That* we hold scripture as authoritative is a given; but in general our tradition has struggled with the implications of *how* it understands and uses the *authority* per se of scripture.[52] Thomas Campbell and others consistently referred to the New Testament as the movement's "constitution," and yet there is far more in the

New Testament literature itself than prescriptions, precepts, and precedents. The New Testament claims authority over us, or as Johnson puts it, "authors our identity"[53] actually more through narratives, and through commandments couched within narratives, than it does through straightforward patterns or injunctions. If we are to discern God's will for the Church, it must come through entering again and again into the narrative world of the New Testament Christians, and thus into the colloquy already going on among the New Testament authorities.[54] For what we find in the New Testament is not a monotonal or monovalent voice, but a polyphony, a diversity of witnesses—reflecting apostolic communities that had significant differences of tradition-history, theological perspective, and religious language and symbolism—which by the grace of God achieved a *consensual* unity of witness, a shared christocentric worldview.

For us, this means that we must gravitate toward what New Testament scripture already affords us as a unifying *center* of Christian identity. Already among the apostolic churches, who were themselves having to interpret the polyphony of Hebrew scripture in the light of the coming of Jesus Christ, there were the makings of a core confession or canonical narrative that the second-century churches called the "Rule of Faith," and which was in later centuries set forth in well tested confessions like the Apostles' Creed.[55] Such a core narrative, the makings of which appear in the New Testament,[56] enshrined in the church's memory that the one God created the world, that he sent his Son in the flesh, who died and was raised for the salvation of all, that God gave his Spirit to the church for the time until Christ the Son would come again to judge the living and the dead. This core narrative ultimately provided the basis for the identity, and the sanctified consensus, of the ancient churches. Lest we immediately throw up the flag of the Stone-Campbell Movement's aversion to creeds, however, it is good to keep in mind that our early-generation leaders already understood that not all of scripture is equally authoritative, that there is a core narrative, the "gospel facts" as Alexander Campbell defined them, which serves as the lens through which we interpret both the Bible *and* our own experience as the church.[57] Indeed, Alexander Campbell was unusually well-disposed toward the Apostles' Creed as evoking the New Testament's own "gospel facts,"[58] and Thomas Campbell too, in one of his later writings, set forth a "Synopsis of Christianity" in which the "gospel facts" closely paralleled clauses from the Apostles' Creed.[59] For the Campbells this kind of *centering* on the evangelical narrative of scripture was a much needed balance to the tendency to reduce New Testament Christianity purely to the patterns and practices of the apostolic churches. Unwittingly perhaps, they were also giving the nod to the fact that the historical tradition of the Church catholic, through such ecumenical confessions as the Apostles' Creed, has provided certain constructive resources for preserving a *consensus fidelium*.

I am pleased that the need of the Stone-Campbell churches to focus on an integrative "core narrative" as the basis of their identity and as a guide to their interpretation of scripture is receiving timely recognition from across the spectrum. Eugene Boring has suggested in his excellent new study of *Disciples and the Bible* that a priority for Disciples must be the recovery of such a core, a rule of faith, for which we can be aided by a catholic confession such as the Apostles' Creed, but even more immediately by our own historic confession of "Jesus Christ" as our creed, that is, commitment to the unique and all-pervasive authority of the person of Jesus Christ, not just to the book that witnesses to him (Robert Richardson revisited!). Boring very constructively recommends a reworking of the mnemonic "Five Finger Exercise" along the lines of a core kerygma of five great facts of the christocentric drama of salvation: Creation, Covenant, Christ, Church, and Consummation.[60]

Similarly Thomas Olbricht, in a splendid autobiographical account of his developing understanding of biblical authority and interpretation in the context of Churches of Christ, has strongly recommended a new "christological," or better yet Trinitarian, rule of faith to be our guide in interpreting the whole of the Bible, such that "commands, examples, and inferences" from scripture are properly situated in the larger narrative of the redemptive work of Father, Son, and Holy Spirit.[61] The same concern is echoed in Richard Hughes's own urgent appeal for a more distinctly *theocentric* hermeneutic in his Reed Lectures. Finally, Frederick Norris and I, from among the Christian Churches and Churches of Christ, have sought to hold up the need for rehabilitating the time-tested ecumenical creeds not as "tests of fellowship" but as doxological pointers to the core kerygma of Christian revelation, the kerygma which will always be basic to a viable *consensus fidelium*.[62]

A hermeneutic that is focused and centered on the "core narrative," our rule of faith, will enable us in the Stone-Campbell churches to authenticate our fidelity to the apostolic tradition and the Church catholic while upholding and adapting our tradition's own distinctive commitments to the contemporary context in which we live. To take the example of sacramentology, it may not be sufficient anymore to recommend our practice of believers' immersion solely through pointing to the philological evidence of *baptizein* and its cognates in the Greek New Testament, or by lining up the scriptural texts that prescribe the "ordinance" of immersion in the *ordo salutis*. These justifications certainly still have value in evangelistic and catechetical contexts, but we are bound to be more persuasive in our witness to the wider Christian community, and to a world wearied of biblical prooftexting, if we let the action of immersion speak for itself as the sacramental drama of our *entry into the death, burial, and resurrection of Jesus Christ*.

Such a perspective frames immersion within the core kerygma of Christianity, the redemptive story that identifies us directly with Jesus Christ and with the church catholic. The same holds true for our practice of the Lord's supper. We can expend all our energies on identifying the scriptural warrants for its regular observance, and so too risk reducing the supper to a mere weekly "ordinance" for memorializing our Lord's past sacrifice. Our witness will be far more compelling, however, if we observe the supper within the full context of the evangelical narrative of our faith, recognizing that through the eucharist Jesus Christ comes to us out of the past *and* out of the future to be personally present with us *now* as Savior and Lord. Indeed, the reality of our encounter with the crucified, risen, and exalted Lord in the supper is itself the single most powerful rationale for its weekly (or even more frequent) celebration.

More difficult, in the discernment process, is the interpretation of the Bible, and the appeal to the core kerygma, in addressing new and controversial issues arising in the life of our churches, be they doctrinal, social or ethical, liturgical, organizational, or whatever. Is our identification with this core narrative strong enough to hold us together and to resist the centrifugal force of significant differences not just of "opinion" but of trained interpretation? The question is an acute one, given the tensions between competing schools of thought that each of the three branches of the Stone-Campbell heritage continues to experience internally, let alone the perspectival and ecclesiological differences separating the three branches from one another. As a number of historians love to remind us, we were the movement that championed the rights of individuals to interpret scripture for themselves, only to divide over the consequences of that freedom.[63] Thus a significant dimension of our movement's historic "discernment process" has been the very learning of an *ecclesial* hermeneutic that cherishes unity in diversity. We are still learning.

As we look to the example of the apostolic churches, though, we can take some comfort from the fact that for Paul himself, the process of *communally* discerning God's will, achieving what Paul calls the "mind of Christ" (1 Cor. 2:16) on a given issue or problem, was rarely an orderly parliamentary process. For Paul and his churches, as Luke Johnson points out, exercising discernment was a risky adventure in reinterpreting scripture in the light of the crucified and risen Christ, while also setting the many "narratives" of Christians' contemporary experience before the touchstone of God's living and active Word.[64] The latter assuredly does *not* mean the rather ill-defined and trendy "storyweaving" so popular in some denominations today, which frequently celebrates diversity of experience as an end in itself, with only the most innocuous expression of unity-amid-difference. Discernment means testing the (sometimes conflicting) paths of human experience in the church that can either edify or tear down its ecclesial vitality and mission. Inevitably it means communal decision-making on tough issues, where reaching a sanctified consensus may entail a lot of stumbling and staggering until insight is reached. Luke Johnson's analysis is particularly appropriate for the Stone-Campbell churches when he writes,

> Most of us would prefer norms more steady and machinery less personal for our decision-making process. But the need for spiritual discernment in the process of reaching decision is derived from the very essence of the church's life. When bylaws and customs, or codes and unreflected Scripture citations replace the testing of the Spirit in the church, or more tragically, when the church proceeds on the assumption that there is no work of the Spirit to *be* tested, then the church may reveal itself in the process of reaching decision, but it won't be as a community of faith in the Spirit.[65]

Always discernment requires a respect for the "otherness" of the text of scripture (its resistance to manipulation), and more importantly the holy otherness of God, whose will is characteristically discerned in its contrariness to human will, so often betraying itself as a weakness or "folly" (cf. 1 Cor. 1:21–25) that runs paradoxically counter to pretentious human judgment.[66] We would do well to learn from the likes of John Cassian and the monastic tradition that true Christian discernment entails agonizing reappraisal, soul-searching, a disciplined asceticism of prayer, patience, the combination of deep conviction and openness to the Spirit of God, on the part of each and every Christian body, congregation, and member.

In closing, I would hasten to add that true discernment is not just a matter of sound judgment concerning present issues and problems; it has a *prospective* and even *visionary* dimension to it. As we discern the will of God for our churches, we are aspiring to set ourselves into God's context, striving to be actors rather than spectators in God's unfolding drama of salvation, and projecting ourselves into God's future, all of which are actions of faith rather than purest sight. The "future vision" of the Stone-Campbell Movement is still being birthed out of its "founding vocation." I hope that this essay has demonstrated that, as we articulate our future vision, we are already having to reinterpret the founding vocation itself, discerning its ramifications for circumstances very different from those of the nineteenth-century American frontier. Revisionist histories can often be abusive and tendentious, but it is inevitable that as we strive to keep the "Current Reformation" current, we necessarily rethink the past for the future. I am convinced that we need not narrowly reduce the founding vocation of the Stone-Campbell Movement to any one founding text (even the *Declaration and Address!*), to any one founder, or to any one commitment. The founding vocation was not a *founding* vocation until it had been tried and tested, until the movement proved some depth and maturity, some ability to pursue a sanctified consensus, some performance in evangelization.

To put it another way, the founding vocation was not frozen in time at any given point; it was a matter of the collective examples of freedom, unity, apostolic fidelity, and missionary commitment being set by a whole "cloud of witnesses" in the movement's past. In fact it was often individuals outside the "founding foursome" who played a critical and prophetic role in shaping the movement: unsung heroes like Robert Richardson, who discerned a genuinely spiritual and eschatological dimension of the restoration principle, or, in the union of 1832, J. T. Johnson and Raccoon John Smith, whose labors were indispensable in forging a consensus between the Stone and Campbell movements.

Ultimately, however, discerning the future vision of the Stone-Campbell Movement rests not only on effective critical appropriation of our past but in constantly holding ourselves and our past up to the standard of the "core kerygma" of our faith. At the very nucleus of that kerygma is Christ crucified and risen, to whom we are *personally* and *ecclesially* accountable. There is much room for penitence. We are not the reincarnation of the "New Testament Church"; our history is in many respects a feeble testament to Christian unity; we are a broken people. But where there is discernment, striving after the "mind of Christ," the cardinal Christian virtues of faith, love, *and hope* must be close at hand; indeed, spiritual growth in these virtues is the precondition for discerning a future vision of Christian unity, apostolic integrity, and global mission. J. H. Garrison's recommendation at the time of the Disciples Centennial still holds good today:

> We may go into permanent camp on a fixed human creed, but with Christ as our creed we must "follow on to know the Lord." We cannot follow Christ as Leader without growing in knowledge of his religion, *and therefore in the power of spiritual discernment.* The liberty to think, and to reach our convictions of duty for ourselves is not more inherent in the plea we are making than the obligation to grow both in grace and in the knowledge of the truth. . . What is true of the individual is true of a religious movement as a whole, which must embody the sum total of the intellectual and spiritual development of its parts. If we fail to recognize the law of spiritual growth as applicable to religious movements as well as to individuals, we might as well grow pessimistic for the future.[67]

NOTES

[1]See note 46 below.

[2]As Anthony Dunnavant indicates in his first lecture, issues of self-definition had already figured prominently in some of the early Reed Lectureships as well.

[3]J. H. Garrison, ed., *The Reformation of the Nineteenth Century* (St. Louis: Christian Publishing, 1901).

[4]J. H. Garrison, *The Story of a Century: A Brief Historical Sketch and Exposition of the Religious Movement Inaugurated by Thomas and Alexander Campbell, 1809–1909* (St. Louis: Christian Publishing, 1909), 263.

[5]Ibid., 247.

[6]On these divergences, see Douglas Foster, "The Many Faces of Christian Unity: Disciples Ecumenism and Schism, 1875–1900," in *Explorations in the Stone-Campbell Traditions: Essays in Honor of Herman A. Norton*, ed. Anthony Dunnavant and Rich-

ard Harrison (Nashville: Disciples of Christ Historical Society, 1995), esp. 95–97.
Dunnavant himself in his first Reed lecture notes the influence of the perspectives
of Hiram Van Kirk, *The Rise of the Current Reformation* (St. Louis: Christian Publishing Co., 1907); and Ronald Osborn, *Experiment in Liberty: The Ideal of Freedom in the
Experience of the Disciples of Christ*, The Reed Lectures 1976 (St. Louis: Bethany Press,
1978).

[7]See most recently, for example, G. Richard Phillips, "Variations in the Major
Themes of Alexander Campbell's Thought: Just Cause for Variations in Interpreta-
tion," in *Explorations in the Stone-Campbell Traditions*, 71–93; and the essays on the
legacies of Barton Stone by Anthony Dunnavant, C. Leonard Allen, and myself in
Cane Ridge in Context: Perspectives on Barton W. Stone and the Revival, ed. Anthony
Dunnavant (Nashville: Disciples of Christ Historical Society, 1992).

[8]I would note that Dunnavant's choice of core commitments here is very close
to that of W. E. Garrison in his *Christian Unity and the Disciples of Christ* (St. Louis:
Bethany Press, 1955), 6–7, who revises the conventional unity/restoration thesis to
focus on conversion or world *evangelization* as the preeminent commitment, effected
through a united Church whose *unity* was grounded in the *restoration of apostolic
authority* and the honoring of *liberty* in matters of human opinion.

[9]Demonstrated, Dunnavant shows, in Alexander Campbell's now famous
"Letter to an Independent Baptist" and Lunenburg correspondence.

[10]Hughes here seems to echo the perspective of Thomas Grafton, who in his
1897 book on Alexander Campbell, suggested that in essence "his mission was that
of a truth-seeker, rather than the advocate of a doctrine," devoted to "an independent search for wisdom" (*Alexander Campbell: Leader of the Great Reformation of the
Nineteenth Century* [St. Louis: Christian Publishing, 1897]), 229.

[11]See especially the influential book of James Robinson and Helmut Koester,
Trajectories through Early Christianity (Philadelphia: Fortress Press, 1971).

[12]See Harnack's Liberal classic *What Is Christianity?* [trans. of *Das Wesen des
Christentums*] (New York: Putnam's, 1901).

[13]Cf. Barton Stone, "Christian Union," in the *Works of Elder B. W. Stone*, ed.
James Mathes (Cincinnati: Moore, Wilstach, Keys, & Co., 1859), 308ff; Thomas
Campbell, *Declaration and Address*, reprinted in *Historical Documents Advocating
Christian Union*, ed. C. H. Young (Chicago: Christian Century, 1904); Alexander
Campbell, *The Christian System*, 4th ed. (Cincinnati: H. S. Bosworth, 1866), 105ff;
Walter Scott, *To Themelion: The Union of Christians on Christian Principles* (Cincinnati:
C. A. Morgan & Co., 1852), esp. 100–128; idem, *He Nekrosis, or the Death of Christ,
Written for the Recovery of the Church from Sects* (Cincinnati: C. A. Morgan & Co.,
1853), esp. 46–47.

[14]See Thomas Campbell, "Christianity is Neither a Theory nor a Philosophy,"
reprinted in Alexander Campbell's *Memoirs of Elder Thomas Campbell* (Cincinnati:
H. S. Bosworth, 1861), 253ff.

[15]Alexander Campbell, *The Christian System*, 17–18.

[16]Ibid., 18.

[17]I am grateful to Prof. Douglas Foster for a manuscript of his responses to Richard
Hughes's Reed Lectures at David Lipscomb University, September 26–27, 1997.

[18]Robert Richardson, "Interpretation of the Scriptures," *Millennial Harbinger*
(1848), 435.

[19]See Henry May, *The Enlightenment in America* (New York: Oxford University
Press, 1976), 337–57.

[20]George Marsden, "Everyone One's Own Interpreter? The Bible, Science, and
Authority in Mid-Nineteenth-Century America," in *The Bible in America: Essays in
Cultural History*, ed. Nathan Hatch and Mark Noll (New York: Oxford University
Press, 1982), 79–100. Also on this bibliocentric cultural consensus, see Grant Wacker,
"The Demise of Biblical Civilization," in *The Bible in America*, esp. 121–22. On the
profound influence of Common Sense philosophy on American Protestantism in
the early- to mid-nineteenth century, see T. Dwight Bozeman, *Protestants in an Age*

of Science: The Baconian Ideal in Antebellum American Religious Thought (Chapel Hill: University of North Carolina Press, 1977); E. Brooks Holifield, *The Gentlemen Theologians: American Theology in Southern Culture 1795–1860* (Durham, N.C.: Duke University Press, 1978), 72–126; and Michael Gauvreau, "The Empire of Evangelicalism: Varieties of Common Sense in Scotland, Canada, and the United States," in *Evangelicalism: Comparative Studies of Popular Protestantism in North America, the British Isles, and Beyond 1700–1990*, ed. Mark Noll, David Bebbington, and George Rawlyk (New York: Oxford University Press, 1994), 219–52.

[21]Thomas Campbell, *Declaration and Address*, reprinted in *Historical Documents Advocating Christian Union*, 97.

[22]Ibid., 95.

[23]On this see Marsden, "Everyone One's Own Interpreter?" 80–81, 93–94.

[24]Richard Hughes has documented very well the incipient attempts to turn restoration into an end in itself, leading to exclusivistic claims that the movement had reconstituted the New Testament church unscathed by the shaping effects of history and tradition. See not only his second lecture above (especially his comments on John Howard and Arthur Crihfield), but his more developed argument in *Reviving the Ancient Faith: The Story of Churches of Christ in America* (Grand Rapids: Eerdmans, 1996), 54–91.

[25]Cf. Robert Richardson, "The Spirit of God," series in the *Millennial Harbinger* 1842–1843; idem (under the pseudonym Silas), "The Crisis," no. 2 *Millennial Harbinger* (1844), 61–62; ibid., no. 4, *Millennial Harbinger* (1844), 272–73.

[26]Robert Richardson, "Faith versus Philosophy," no. 2, *Millennial Harbinger* (1857), 191–97.

[27]Ibid., no. 5, *Millennial Harbinger* (1857), 333; cf. idem, "Misinterpretation of Scripture," no. 1, *Millennial Harbinger* (1856), 503. See also idem, "Faith and Philosophy," no. 6, *Millennial Harbinger* (1857), 493, where Richardson openly reprehends this empiricist philosophy as having "cramped the energies and arrested the advance of this religious movement to some extent..."

[28]Robert Richardson, "Faith versus Philosophy," no. 5, *Millennial Harbinger* (1857), 396–97; cf. idem, "Misinterpretation of Scripture," no. 1, *Millennial Harbinger* (1856), 504–5.

[29]See Richardson's dismay about overconfidence in the "plainness" of the scriptures in "Misinterpretation of Scripture," no. 1, *Millennial Harbinger* (1856): 502ff; also idem, "Interpretation of the Scriptures," no. 11, *Millennial Harbinger* (1849), 267, where Richardson castigates "wordy harangues upon the plainness of the scriptures" and the "rage for simplification."

[30]Robert Richardson, "Faith versus Philosophy," no. 5, *Millennial Harbinger* (1857), 400–403, 405–6.

[31]Ibid., no. 5, *Millennial Harbinger* (1857), 336, 402–4; cf. ibid., no. 7, *Millennial Harbinger* (1857), 551. For Coleridge's views on "bibliolatry" (a term he ostensibly picked up from the eighteenth-century writer John Byrom), see his *Confessions of an Inquiring Spirit*, 3rd ed. (1853) (reprint ed., Philadelphia: Fortress Press, 1988), 42, 61.

[32]Robert Richardson, "Faith versus Philosophy," no. 9, *Millennial Harbinger* (1857), 692–93.

[33]See Lyman Beecher's famous address "A Plea for the West" (2nd ed., 1835), reprinted in excerpted form in *God's New Israel: Religious Interpretations of America's Destiny*, ed. Conrad Cherry (Englewood Cliffs, N.J.: Prentice-Hall, 1971), 119–27.

[34]Some of these factors are analyzed in detail by Wacker, "The Demise of Biblical Civilization," 122–33. Timothy Weber speaks of a "paradigm shift" in the world of science from a Baconian model to a Darwinist evolutionary one in the later nineteenth and early twentieth centuries. Truth came increasingly to be seen less as immutable or mechanical than as "organic." See his "The Two-Edged Sword: The Fundamentalist Use of the Bible," in *The Bible in America*, esp. 103–4.

³⁵See also Dunnavant's appraisal of this shift and its implications for Disciple organization in his "Restructure: Four Historical Ideals in the Campbell-Stone Movement and the Development of the Polity of the Christian Church (Disciples of Christ)," (Ph.D. diss., Vanderbilt University, 1984), esp. 295–369.

³⁶Harvey W. Everest, "God's Purpose in the Ages," reprinted in *New Testament Christianity*, ed. Z. T. Sweeney (Columbus, Ind.: private publisher, 1923), vol. 1, 290–91. Everest was president of Butler University from 1881 to 1887 and finished his career as Dean of the Bible department at Drake University. I have been unable to locate the precise year in which Everest delivered this sermon, but clearly it comes from the last quarter of the nineteenth century.

³⁷Ibid., 291–93.

³⁸Ibid., 296.

³⁹Garrison, *The Story of a Century*, 273, 274, 275.

⁴⁰See D. Newell Williams, ed., *A Case Study of Mainstream Protestantism: The Disciples' Relation to American Culture, 1880–1989* (Grand Rapids: Eerdmans, 1991); cf. also Ronald Osborn, "The Irony of the Twentieth-Century Christian Church (Disciples of Christ): Making It to the Mainline Just at the Time of Its Disestablishment," *Mid-Stream* 28 (July 1989), 293–312.

⁴¹On the "Independents," see in particular G. Richard Phillips, "From Modern Theology to a Post-Modern World: Christian Churches and Churches of Christ," *Discipliana* 54 (1994), 83–95; Henry Webb, *In Search of Christian Unity: A History of the Restoration Movement* (Cincinnati: Standard Publishing, 1990), esp. 249–360, 423–34; and James North, *Union in Truth: An Interpretive History of the Restoration Movement* (Cincinnati: Standard Publishing, 1994), esp. 289–369. There have been some constructive initiatives, however, including the recent open forums between representatives of the Christian Churches and the Churches of God (Anderson, Indiana): see Barry Callen and James North, eds., *Coming Together in Christ: Pioneering a New Testament Way to Christian Unity* (Joplin, Mo.: College Press, 1997).

⁴²See especially his larger study, *Reviving the Ancient Faith;* cf. also Douglas Foster, *Will the Cycle Be Unbroken? Churches of Christ Face the 21st Century* (Abilene, Tex.: Abilene Christian University Press, 1994).

⁴³Garrison, *The Story of a Century*, 264–65.

⁴⁴John Theil, *Nonfoundationalism*, Guides to Theological Inquiry series (Minneapolis: Augsburg Fortress, 1994), 42. Theil's study provides an excellent introductory survey of the manifestations of Nonfoundationalism in contemporary philosophy and theology.

⁴⁵See ibid., esp. 38–78.

⁴⁶The studies coming out of the Disciples of Christ Historical Society's Forrest-Kirkpatrick Seminar for 1994–96, on the theme of "A Nineteenth-Century Religious Movement Faces the Twenty-First Century," have been quite useful and thought provoking. From the perspective of the Christian Church (Disciples of Christ), see Clark Williamson, "Confusions in Disciple Talk and Practice: Theology in the Life of the Church," *Discipliana* 55 (1995), 3–13; Brenda Brasher, "The Christian Church (Disciples of Christ): Into the Third Millennium," *Discipliana* 55 (1995), 81–94; and Daisy Machado, "From Anglo-American Traditions to a Multicultural World," *Discipliana* 57 (1997), 47–60. From the perspective of the Christian Churches and Churches of Christ, see G. Richard Phillips, "From Modern Theology to a Post-Modern World: Christian Churches and Churches of Christ," *Discipliana* 54 (1994), 83–95; Byron C. Lambert, "From Rural Churches to an Urban World: Shifting Frontiers and the Invisible Hand," *Discipliana* 55 (1995), 67–80; and Rondal Smith, "The Independent Christian Churches Face a Multicultural Twenty-First Century," *Discipliana* 57 (1997), 35–46. And from the perspective of the Churches of Christ, see Kathy Pulley, "The Churches of Christ: Accommodation to Modernity and the Challenges of Post-Modernity," *Discipliana* 54 (1994), 109–19; Gary Holloway and Michael Weed, "The Gospel in Urban Vessels: Churches of Christ Face the Twenty-First

Century," *Discipliana* 55 (1995), 109–21; and Dewayne Winrow, "Multiculturalism in Churches of Christ," *Discipliana* 57 (1997), 67–79. Cf. also some other relevant studies reflecting similar critical interests: Ronald Osborn, "The Irony of the Twentieth-Century Christian Church (Disciples of Christ): Making It to the Mainline Just at the Time of Its Disestablishment," *Mid-Stream* 28 (July 1989), 293–312; D. Newell Williams, ed., *A Case Study of Mainstream Protestantism: The Disciples' Relation to American Culture, 1880–1989* (Grand Rapids: Eerdmans, 1991); Mark Toulouse, *Joined in Discipleship*, 2nd ed. (St. Louis: Chalice Press, 1997); Robert Fife, "The Stone-Campbell Movement: Toward a Responsible Future," in *Celebration of Heritage* (Los Angeles: Westwood Christian Foundation, 1992), 443–62; Douglas Foster, *Will the Cycle Be Unbroken? Churches of Christ Face the 21st Century* (Abilene, Tex.: Abilene Christian University Press, 1994); and C. Leonard Allen, *The Cruciform Church: Becoming a Cross-Shaped People in a Secular World* (Abilene, Tex.: Abilene Christian University Press, 1990).

[47]On this reconfiguration, and most notably the transitions in mainline Protestantism, there are numerous recent analyses, but see in particular Philip Hammond, *Religion and Personal Autonomy: The Third Disestablishment in America* (Columbia: University of South Carolina Press, 1992); Robert Wuthnow, *The Restructuring of American Religion* (Princeton: Princeton University Press, 1988); Wade Clark Roof and William McKinney, *American Mainline Religion* (New Brunswick, N.J.: Rutgers University Press, 1987); Jackson Carroll and Wade Clark Roof, *Beyond Establishment: Protestant Identity in a Post-Protestant Age* (Louisville: Westminster John Knox Press, 1993); Milton Coalter, John Mulder, and Louis Weeks, *Vital Signs: The Promise of Mainstream Protestantism* (Grand Rapids: Eerdmans, 1996); Randall Balmer, *Grant Us Courage: Travels Along the Mainline of American Protestantism* (New York: Oxford University Press, 1996); Thomas Robbins and Dick Anthony, eds., *In God We Trust: New Patterns in Religious Pluralism in America*, 2nd ed. (New Brunswick, N.J.: Transaction Publications, 1990), esp. the essays in Section III.

[48]He also mentions the important "Process of Discernment" document drafted for the Disciples' General Assembly at Pittsburgh in 1995. See the text in the *Business Docket and Program: General Assembly, Christian Church Disciples of Christ*, Pittsburgh, Penn., Oct. 20–24, 1995. Cf. also two recent documents published by the Office of the General Minister and President: "Reflections on 'Discernment' for the Christian Church (Disciples of Christ)," prepared by Rev. Lori Adams; and "The Process of Discernment on the Nature of Biblical Authority for the Christian Church (Disciples of Christ)," prepared by an ad hoc Commission on Discernment for Biblical Authority. Both of these latter texts have been made available on the internet home page of the Christian Church (Disciples of Christ): http://www.disciples.org.

[49]Robert Richardson, "Misinterpretation of Scripture," no. 1, *Millennial Harbinger* (1856), 503–4.

[50]John Cassian (d. 435), *Conferences* (Conference 2: "On Discernment"), trans. Colm Luibheid, *Classics of Western Spirituality* (New York: Paulist Press, 1985), 60.

[51]Luke Timothy Johnson, *Scripture and Discernment: Decision-Making in the Church*, revised ed. (Nashville: Abingdon Press, 1996), esp. chaps. 2 and 6.

[52]There was a time when simply claiming to stand on "the Bible, the whole Bible, and nothing but the Bible" (Alexander Campbell, *The Christian System*, 104) seemed sufficient in itself; today it is a claim that must be nuanced more discreetly. Campbell, of course, had already begun to do that, as had his father, in setting forth the superior authority of the New Testament and of its "gospel facts" (see below, 57).

[53]See Johnson, *Scripture and Discernment*, 40–41.

[54]See ibid., 42–43.

[55]See my essay "The *Regula Fidei* and the Narrative Character of Early Christian Faith," *Pro Ecclesia* 6 (1997), 199–228.

[56]Cf. Acts 2:14–39; 3:13–26; 4:10–12; 5:30–32; 10:36–43; 13:17–41; Rom. 1:1–4; 2:16; 4:24; 8:34; 10:8–9; 1 Cor. 8:6; 15:1–7; Gal. 1:3–4; 3:1; 1 Thess. 1:10; 1 Tim. 3:16;

6:13–16; 2 Tim. 2:8; 1 Peter 1:21; 3:18ff; see also C. H. Dodd's still classic *The Apostolic Preaching and Its Developments*, new ed. (London: Hodder & Stoughton, 1944).
[57]See *The Christian System*, chap. 23 ("Summary View of the Christian System of Facts"), 71–72; cf. ibid., 111, where Campbell focuses on the most central of these "gospel facts":

> To enumerate the gospel facts would be to narrate all that is recorded of the sayings and doings of Jesus Christ from his birth to his coronation in the heavens. They are, however, concentrated in a few prominent ones, which group together all the love of God in the gift of his Son. He died for our sin she was buried in the grave he rose from the dead for our justification and is ascended to the skies to prepare mansions for his disciples comprehend the whole, or are the heads of the chapters which narrate the love of God and display his moral majesty and glory to our view.

On this core gospel as the key to Campbell's own understanding of Christian identity, see also the insightful remarks of D. Newell Williams in his concluding essay to *A Case Study of Mainstream Protestantism*, 563–65.
[58]See Alexander Campbell, "Reply to Barnabas," *Millennial Harbinger* (1832), 602, where Campbell writes of the Apostles' Creed: "...I can say, *ex animo*, that I believe every word of it. Because it is not, like all modern creeds, a synopsis of opinions, but a brief narrative of facts, and of all the great gospel facts."
[59]Thomas Campbell, "Synopsis of Christianity," *Millennial Harbinger* (1844), 481–91.
[60]Eugene Boring, *Disciples and the Bible: A History of Disciples Biblical Interpretation in North America* (St. Louis: Chalice Press, 1997), 429–46.
[61]Thomas Olbricht, *Hearing God's Voice: My Life with Scripture in the Churches of Christ* (Abilene, Tex.: Abilene Christian University Press, 1996), esp. 274ff, 289–90, 335–37, 347–56, 382–92.
[62]Frederick Norris, *The Apostolic Faith: Protestants and Roman Catholics* (Collegeville, Minn.: Liturgical Press, 1992). In urging the constructive use of the Nicene Creed, Norris is not exclusively addressing the Stone-Campbell churches, but he *is* also speaking to our churches. My own work on the early Christian *regula fidei* and the Apostles' Creed (see note 55) is more a historical-theological study than a direct appeal to the use of the Apostles' Creed among Christian Churches and Churches of Christ. Nevertheless, my description of the *regula* and the Creed as evangelical "metanarratives" is intended to indicate their profitability for all contemporary churches questing for apostolic integrity and a viable unity-in-diversity.
[63]E.g., Nathan Hatch, "*Sola Scriptura* and *Novus Ordo Seclorum*," in *The Bible in America*, esp. 71–75; and more recently his *The Democratization of American Christianity* (New Haven: Yale University Press, 1989), esp. 70–81, 162–89.
[64]See Johnson, *Scripture and Discernment*, 41–44, 51–58, 136–39.
[65]Ibid., 138.
[66]Ibid., 53–54, 127–29.
[67]Garrison, *The Story of a Century*, 244 (emphasis added).

CHAPTER 6

Discernment among the Heirs of Stone and the Campbells

Anthony L. Dunnavant

In "Keeping the 'Current Reformation' Current" Paul Blowers has written a response that honors the Reed Lectures for 1995 and 1997 by the generosity of his assessment. More significantly, however, he has offered his own helpful analysis of the issue that engaged the lecturers, that of the diverging self-understandings of the Stone-Campbell traditions.

It is noteworthy that an early twentieth-century work by J. H. Garrison supplies the guiding image for Blowers's essay. Because there is always a temptation to seek to appropriate the words and identities of founding figures for the support of one's own point of view, it is salutary to recall the wisdom of the second and subsequent generations of one's tradition. By resisting the urge to leap over those whose experiences and reflections intervened between the founders and ourselves we are availed the benefit of learning from those whose historical location is more akin to ours than is that of the founders. Garrison and the members of his generation were, like us, religious heirs of Stone and the Campbells, recipients of a tradition that was confronting a changed and changing social, historical, and theological context.

As we stand on the threshold of the twenty-first century, a growing edge in the historiography of the Stone-Campbell traditions remains the further exploration of the theological transitions that took place near the turn of the past century. Commenting on the Disciples' transition "from rational supernaturalism" to "post-Kantian liberalism," James O. Duke has noted that "its long-term aftereffects have included mass confusion about 'the theological identity' of the Christian Church (Disciples of Christ)."[1] Intellectual history is no guaranteed antidote for such "mass confusion," but neglecting the history virtually guarantees the continuity of the confusion. Therefore, Blowers and Duke do well in reminding us of the "transitional" reflections of Garrison and W. T. Moore as a way into deepened critical thought about our own self-understandings as a religious people in changing times.

Further, Blowers provides a typology, drawn by analogy from New Testament studies, which contrasts the "trajectory-critical" with the "singular essence" modes of defining the Stone-Campbell Movement. This does seem to illuminate not only differences in the *accounts* of the Stone-Campbell traditions offered by Richard Hughes and me, but, more importantly, *real underlying differences* between the constituent memberships of the Churches of Christ and Christian Church (Disciples of Christ) with regard to their predominant self-understandings. Therefore, the typology does offer potential critical insight into the strengths and vulnerabilities associated with each of these contrasting approaches to self-definition. In the case of the Christian Church (Disciples of Christ) there does seem to be a vulnerability that has to do with the elusiveness of "a final touchstone of *normative* self-definition" among us who understand ourselves to be on a "journey."[2]

Blowers goes beyond his helpful and provocative identification of the "trajectory-critical" versus "singular essence" understandings of the Stone-Campbell traditions. He offers a third approach that emphasizes "the core kerygma of Christian revelation," which is pointed to "doxologically" in the "time-tested ecumenical creeds" and "narratively" in the biblical "Christocentric drama of salvation." It is a welcome and hopeful sign that Blowers does *not* press the claims of this constructive proposal in terms of its being the mediating position of his own communion, the undenominational fellowship of Christian Churches and Churches of Christ. He does not present it as that fellowship's obvious alternative to the "trajectory-critical" approach of the Christian Church (Disciples of Christ) on the one hand and to the "singular essence" approach of the Churches of Christ on the other. Rather, he identifies voices in each of the three alienated branches of the Stone-Campbell heritage who seem to him to be calling for the kind of "focus on an integrative 'core narrative'" of Christian faith that he advocates. In this connection, Frederick Norris of his own fellowship, M. Eugene Boring of the Christian Church (Disciples of Christ), and Thomas Olbricht of the Churches of Christ are mentioned appreciatively as having contributed to this "third way." This makes clear that Professor Blowers is seeking to do more than add a third voice to a trio and to do other than assert his own as the dominant voice.

Paul Blowers' strong affirmation of the value of discernment should come as both a word of encouragement and of caution to those of us in the Christian Church (Disciples of Christ) who have been called to a formal and structured discernment process and to all Christians who would claim to be discerning. If alleged discernment consistently yields only those words and actions that arise predictably from one's prior social and ideological location, the process will rightly be regarded with skepticism and, ultimately, dismissed with cynicism. Nevertheless, it is encouraging to encounter Paul Blowers' richly textured discussion of discernment and its biblical and patristic meanings alongside his persuasive statement of its importance in the contemporary church. Blowers' statement, in the company of others such as that recently made by Ruth Fletcher, gives rise to the anticipation that discernment may, indeed, have more to do with "faith" than with "fad," and so hold high promise for the church in our times.[3]

The promise of discernment, of becoming aware of and responsive to the leading of God's Spirit, may require a higher level of honesty and self-critical awareness than that to which we have grown accustomed. Richard Hamm, the General Minister and President of the Christian Church (Disciples of Christ), has linked the issue of discernment to the need for churches to "gain release from the bondage of culture."[4] If we are to take that need seriously, it may mean learning to be critical of "our" as well as "their" form of acculturation. That is, isn't it true that the leadership, and (to a far lesser degree) membership, of the Christian Church (Disciples of Christ) (and its antecedent "cooperative Disciples") have lived much of the twentieth century in relation to an old-line Protestant liberalism that is especially vulnerable to becoming acculturated to, if not indistinguishable from, an amorphous but unmistakably culturally codified Left? Likewise, hasn't the leadership, and (perhaps to a greater degree) membership, of the fellowship of Christian Churches and of the Churches of Christ lived much of the twentieth century in relation to an evangelical Protestantism that is especially vulnerable to becoming acculturated to a similarly amorphous but unmistakably culturally codified Right? If formal and informal processes of discernment lead only to Left-Wing-friendly results among Disciples and only to Right-Wing-friendly results among Christian Churches and Churches of Christ, the suspicion that claims of discernment are actually conscious or unconscious subterfuge will, quite legitimately, arise.

This rather grim observation is not meant to discourage the efforts at discernment, but to signal how much is at stake. In an era when many of our children can explore cyberspace, mass media, and "social space" with very little constraint and few filters, discernment of many sorts is desperately needed. In an era when at least one of the trends of congregational life among Christians is experimentation away from the particularities of scriptural, liturgical, confessional, and catechetical language toward the generic and inoffensive, discernment is needed. We should just not be naive about discernment's being simple or easy.

Perhaps the very need for, and difficulty of, discernment points to a dimension of our "founding vocation" in the Stone-Campbell traditions to which we are now challenged to recommit. We were born as a people to use our God-given freedom to seek the unity of the body of Christ, on the foundation of the apostles' teachings, that the world might believe. Historic, structural *differentiations* on the Left among old-line liberal churches and on the Right among conservative-evangelical churches have for more than half a century now been less significant than the real *division* between these two broad camps, clusters, or "parties" within (and even a bit beyond) Protestantism in the United States. In the Stone-Campbell traditions we have three communions that manifest, at least in part, that deep division and, yet, who share a unitive vocation. Is there hope that God may allow some among us to discern a way of being Christian that transcends participation in this contemporary division with our respective temptations to acculturation? I hope so.

I was made hopeful by the powerful prophetic voice of Richard Hughes who, in his first 1997 Reed Lecture, stated eloquently his fellowship's rootage in the radical vision of Christian freedom glimpsed by Barton Stone. Yet more productive of hope, however, was Hughes's second lecture because its call for ecclesiastical humility on the part of his own fellowship in relation to its "undenominational" self-understanding was a word that could be easily and wholesomely applied to every Christian communion in relation to some point of pride. The experience of being present and hearing Richard Hughes courageously tell a painful truth to a particular church he loves, on behalf of a whole church he loves, was an unforgettable and profound blessing. I hope that the readers of this volume may receive something of that blessing as well.

Finally, what Richard Hughes has called his hearers (and readers) to is a humble, realistic, historical self-consciousness. His comment is apt for the entire family of the Stone-Campbell traditions—"ours is a finite movement and not the fullness of the Kingdom of God." Historical reflection and dialogue helps us in our recognition of our finitude and of our sinfulness. It helps, too, in our recommitment to Christian vocation and our recapturing of Christian vision. For the opportunity that the Disciples of Christ Historical Society gave, in the providence of God, to participants in the Reed Lectures for reflectively recommitting to the founding vocation and for catching a glimpse of a future vocation for the Stone-Campbell traditions, I give thanks to the Society, to my partners in the work, and to our God.

NOTES

[1] James O. Duke, "The Nineteenth-Century Reformation in Historical-Theological Perspective: The First One Hundred Years," in *Christian Faith Seeking Historical Understanding: Essays in Honor of H. Jack Forstman*, ed. James O. Duke and Anthony L. Dunnavant (Macon, Ga.: Mercer University Press, 1997), 184–86.

[2] You will recognize, of course, this term as drawn from the title of Lester G. McAllister and William E. Tucker, *Journey in Faith: A History of the Christian Church (Disciples of Christ)* (St. Louis: Bethany Press, 1975).

[3] See Ruth Fletcher's "Discernment: Faith or Fad?" *Impact: A Journal of the Thought of Disciples of Christ on the Pacific Slope* 39 (1997), 1–14, for a helpful brief treatment of the biblical, patristic, reformation, and contemporary Christian meanings of discernment. Fletcher's article also sets the model for discernment adopted at the 1997 General Assembly of the Christian Church (Disciples of Christ). The author concludes with a theological reflection on discernment.

[4] Donald D. Reisinger and Mary Anne Parrott, "Foreword," *Impact: A Journal of the Thought of Disciples on the Pacific Slope* 39 (1997), i.

CHAPTER 7

Reflections on the Theme of "Christian Freedom"

Richard T. Hughes

In his assessment of the Forrest Reed Lectures of 1995 and 1997, Professor Paul Blowers has offered an extraordinarily thoughtful and provocative essay, and I am profoundly grateful for his insights.

Future Vision

Those who planned these lectures a number of years ago asked Professor Dunnavant and me to reflect on two specific dimensions of the Stone/Campbell tradition: "founding vocation" and "future vision." While I sought to address both these dimensions, I was particularly concerned to address the latter. There is not much we can do to change the past, but there is much we can do to change the future, and for this reason I was especially grateful for the opportunity to address the question of the "future vision" of the Churches of Christ. As far as I am concerned, therefore, the most critical section of my two lectures appears in the last half of lecture two under the heading, "How Did We Lose Our Way? How Can We Find Our Way Home?" The entirety of the first lecture and the first part of the second lecture constitute an effort to set up a structure that would allow me to develop this final section. The fact that I felt, and continue to feel, so passionately about the future of the Churches of Christ, and therefore about this final section of lecture two, explains why I cast both lectures more in the form of a sermon than in the form of a scholarly treatise.

Yet, insofar as my own presentations are concerned, Professor Blowers focused his comments exclusively on the question of "founding vocation." To this extent, my lectures and his response are like ships passing in the night.

I earnestly wish that Professor Blowers had explored with me the theological implications of what I regard as the very crucial issues I sought to raise in that final section. In the context of the Churches of Christ, for example, what are the theological implications of acknowledging or failing to acknowledge our own finitude? Of acknowledging or failing to acknowledge our own history? Of acknowledging or failing to acknowledge that we do, in fact, have a theology that is not necessarily identical with the biblical text? Of acknowledging or failing to acknowledge that the Churches of Christ just might constitute a denomination, in spite of all our claims to the contrary? The fact that he did not assess these themes may be rooted in that once Professor Blowers moves beyond the founding generation, he does virtually nothing in his comments with the Churches of Christ, focusing instead on the history of the Disciples of Christ and, to some small extent, on the Christian Churches/Churches of Christ.

Founding Vocation

At the same time, I have found extremely helpful and insightful the comments and criticisms Professor Blowers offers with respect to my treatment of the "founding vocation" of the Stone-Campbell tradition. Surely he is correct in pointing out that the "founding vocation" was multifaceted, not unidimensional, a point that I acknowledge in these lectures on more than one occasion and develop at considerable length in *Reviving the Ancient Faith*.

Theological Reflections

Yet, I would still contend that in the minds of the founders of this movement, a preoccupation with the lordship of Almighty God stood prior to any other theme they embraced. Why did they seek to restore the faith and practice of the ancient Christian churches? At the most fundamental possible level, they did so because they sought to respond to the will of God. And why did they seek to demolish the walls of division that separated Christians from one another? Once again, they believed that division in the body of Christ was wrong because God had pronounced it sinful. If their fundamental point of reference was not God, but restoration or unity or evangelism or all these themes taken together, then we may rightly ask in what sense the founding vocation of the Stone Campbell movement was in any sense religious, much less uniquely Christian.

And yet, although we can agree that the founders of our movement responded first of all to God and only secondarily to these lesser concerns, we are faced with the dilemma that they spoke far more often of restoration, unity, and evangelism than they did of God Himself. The truth is, our founders were practical reformers, not theologians. This point becomes especially evident when we compare our founders with, say, Calvin or Luther for whom the reality of God stood quite explicitly at the center of their thought, their oral presentations, and their written texts. In contrast, biblical forms, biblical structures, and biblical procedures dominated the thought, the oral presentations, and the written texts of our founders, especially Alexander Campbell.

Professor Blowers is therefore absolutely correct when he notes that Stone and Campbell seldom spoke explicitly of the sovereignty of God or the finitude of human kind. But did their failure to speak of these categories mean that they did not acknowledge the legitimacy of these themes, at least implicitly?

I am convinced that we find implicit acknowledgment of these themes, especially in the rhetoric our founders employed regarding Christian freedom. When Campbell, Stone, and other leaders of our movement rejected creeds and confessions of faith, or when they argued that every person had the right to search scripture for himself or for herself, or when they rejected the right of the clergy to define dogma for their followers, they implicitly acknowledged that God alone is God and all humanity is fallen. No one, they claimed, had a corner on the market of truth, and no one had the right to set himself in the seat of God.

Put another way, while our founders were practical reformers and not theologians, and while they seldom spoke in explicit terms regarding the sovereignty of God or the finitude of humankind, it seems to me that their language regarding Christian freedom reflected deep convictions in this regard. Further, of all the categories of interest to the founders—restoration, unity, mission, and freedom—their convictions about Christian freedom uniquely possessed the ability to give expression to their beliefs regarding the god-ness of God and the human-ness of humankind.

Clearly, in their preoccupation with the motifs of restoration and unity, the founders responded to the sovereign will of God. But these two themes said nothing about the frailty and finitude of humankind and, in fact, allowed the founders, and especially their followers in later generations, to imagine that through the sheer dent of human effort, they could restore the ancient church and/or unify the kingdom of God. Put another way, the themes of restoration and unity, insofar as they summoned up intense human effort, allowed the founders to indulge themselves in the illusion of human self-sufficiency. Recognition of this fact underscores Professor Blowers' point that even though the founders had their roots in the Reformed side of the Protestant Reformation, illusions of self-sufficiency often tempered in their imaginations the classic Protestant and fundamentally biblical themes of divine sovereignty and human frailty.

Of all the motifs important to the founding vocation of our movement, therefore, only the doctrine of Christian freedom consistently pointed to both sides of the Christian gospel: the sovereignty of God and the finitude of humankind. Clearly, the notion of *human freedom* possesses the potential to exalt human self-sufficiency with a vengeance and routinely does so in American popular culture. But Campbell, Stone, and the other founders of our movement were not so interested in notions of *human freedom* as they were in the theme of *Christian freedom*. According to the doctrine of *Christian* freedom, Christians must continually be free to search the Scripture for further truth since, as finite mortals, they are inevitably given to partial glimpses and distorted understandings. This, it seems to me, is what Alexander Campbell had in mind when he wrote, "I have endeavored to read the scriptures as though no one had read them before me; and I am as much on my guard against reading them today, through the medium of my own views yesterday, or a week ago, as I am against being influenced by any foreign name, authority, or system, whatever."

I certainly am not claiming that the doctrine of Christian freedom was or is identical with the Christian gospel or in any way substitutes for the Christian gospel. Nor do I claim that when Campbell and Stone argued for Christian freedom, they explicitly had in mind the gospel categories of the sovereignty of God and the finitude of humankind. But I do claim that of all the themes important to the founding generation, the doctrine of Christian freedom uniquely symbolized the gospel truths of divine sovereignty and human frailty, though it did so both implicitly and imperfectly.

In part, this is why I have argued in the two presentations in this book that the notion of Christian freedom stood prior to any other category we associate with the founding vocation of the Stone-Campbell Movement. Further, in a movement that has been so attracted to the illusion of human self-sufficiency, we in our generation must latch hold of any motif in the history of our movement that had the power then—and has the power now—to point believers to the gospel truths of the sovereignty of God and the finitude of humankind. Augustine, Luther, and Calvin spoke of these themes explicitly. For the most part, our founders did so only implicitly, most often through their emphasis on Christian freedom. For this reason alone, the theme of Christian freedom is an extraordinarily precious theme in the heritage of the Stone-Campbell tradition.

Historical Reflections

To this point, I have made only a theological argument, not a historical one. The question still begs to be answered, Was the doctrine of Christian freedom as central historically to the founding vocation of our movement as I have suggested in these two lectures? Professor Blowers has his doubts and marshals most of his evidence from the literature that stands on the Campbell side of our movement. Frankly, he may well be right with reference to Alexander Campbell, but in my judgment, he is most certainly mistaken with reference to Barton W. Stone.

I argued at some length in *Reviving the Ancient Faith* that "one could make the case with considerable justification…that the theme of freedom constituted the very heart of the Stoneites' message." One need only recall that for almost a quarter of a century prior to Alexander Campbell's arrival in Kentucky in 1823, the Stoneites guarded their Christian freedom so jealously that they refused to develop any sort of orthodox theology, standard liturgy, or ecclesiastical structure whatsoever. Indeed, in the name of Christian freedom, Barton Stone and many of his followers resisted orthodoxies at virtually every step along the way. When, at an early date, many members of Churches of Christ began to claim that the gifts of the Holy Spirit had ceased with the apostles, the Stoneites rigorously guarded their freedom to remain open to the free movement of the Spirit of God. And when many in the Campbell side of the movement began to make immersion for the remission of sins the sine qua non of membership in the kingdom of God, Stone objected in no uncertain terms.

> Should they make their own peculiar view of immersion a term of fellowship, it will be impossible for them to repel, successfully, the imputation of being sectarians, and of having an authoritative creed (though not written) of one article at least, which is formed of their own opinion of truth; and this short creed would exclude more christians from union than any creed with which I am acquainted.[1]

I quoted in lecture two what I regard as the classic statement from Stone regarding Christian freedom, the sovereignty of God, and the finitude of humankind, but the statement is so important that it bears repeating here.

> We must be fully persuaded, that all uninspired men are fallible, and therefore liable to err...Luther, in a coarse manner, said *that every man was born with a Pope in his belly.* By which I suppose he meant, that every man deemed himself infallible...If the present generation remain under the influence of [this]...principle, the consequences must be, that the spirit of free enquiry will die—our liberty lie prostrated at the feet of ecclesiastical demagogues...[2]

Though Stone supported the restoration of the faith and practice of the ancient Christian church, the restoration agenda almost always took second place to his passion for Christian freedom. And because he cared so deeply about Christian freedom, he resisted sterile orthodoxies and could therefore emerge as an eloquent advocate of Christian unity, even in the face of Christian diversity. In these ways, the doctrine of Christian freedom did, indeed, stand at the heart of those early Churches of Christ that acknowledged the leadership of Barton W. Stone.

NOTES

[1]Barton W. Stone, *Christian Messenger* (August 1830), 201.
[2]Stone, *Christian Messenger* (November 25, 1826), 2.